Lucid Dreaming

Lucid Dreaming

A Concise Guide to Awakening in Your Dreams and in Your Life

STEPHEN LABERGE, PH.D.

sounds true
BOULDER, COLORADO

Sounds True, Inc., Boulder, CO 80306
© 2004, 2009 Stephen LaBerge

Published 2009

Cover and book design by Levi Stephen
Music by Aron Arnold
Printed in the United States of America

ISBN 978-1-59179-675-6

Library of Congress Control Number: 2006921133

20 19 18 17 16 15 14 13

Contents

...

Acknowledgments

...

"When eating fruit, think of the
person who planted the tree."
— VIETNAMESE PROVERB

...

We little know how much we owe to our predecessors; without the efforts of countless others, this work could not have been accomplished. Thanks to them all, known and unknown.

Foremost of those to whom I wish to express my loving gratitude are my parents, Dorothy and Vincent—and their ancestors—*sine quibus non*. Lynne Levitan contributed substantially to the writing of the material, while Patricia "Ki-Lin" Keelin tirelessly and cheerfully edited and tracked down innumerable details. The whole crew at Sounds True was wonderful to work with, patient, thoughtful, and professional, notably Matt Licata, Tami Simon, Mitchell Clute, Randy Roark, and Karen Polaski. I thank them all!

Thanks also to Kenny Felder, Dominick Attisani, the Fetzer Institute, and the Institute for Noetic Studies for financial support.

Finally, I am grateful to Mushkil Gusha for the usual contributions, and ultimately to the person who planted the tree!

1

In Dreams Awake

"Why, sometimes before breakfast, I've believed
as many as six impossible things."
—THE WHITE QUEEN,
THROUGH THE LOOKING GLASS
(LEWIS CARROLL)

. . .

THE WONDERS OF LUCID DREAMING

I realized I was dreaming. I raised my arms and began to rise (actually, I was being lifted). I rose through black sky that blended to indigo, to deep purple, to lavender, to white, then to very bright light. All the time I was being lifted there was the most beautiful music I have ever heard. It seemed like voices rather than instruments. There are no words to describe the JOY I felt. I was very gently lowered back to earth. I had the feeling that I had come to a turning point in my life and I had chosen the right path. The dream, the joy I experienced, was kind of a reward, or so I felt. It was a long, slow slide back to wakefulness with the music echoing in my ears. The euphoria lasted several days; the memory, forever.

—A.F., Bay City, Michigan

I was standing in a field in an open area when my wife pointed in the direction of the sunset. I looked at it and thought, "How odd, I've never seen colors like that before." Then it dawned on me: "I must be dreaming!" Never had I experienced such clarity and perception—the colors were so beautiful and the sense of freedom so exhilarating that I started racing through this beautiful golden wheat field waving my hands in the air and yelling at the top of my voice, "I'm dreaming! I'm dreaming!" Suddenly, I started to lose the dream; it must have been the excitement. I instantly woke up. As it dawned on me what had just happened, I woke my wife and said, "I did it, I did it!" I was conscious within the dream state and I'll never be the same. Funny, isn't it? How a taste of it can affect one like that. It's the freedom I guess; we see that we truly are in control of our own universe.

—D.W., Elk River, Minnesota

As I wandered through a high-vaulted corridor deep within a mighty citadel, I paused to admire the magnificent architecture. Somehow the contemplation of these majestic surroundings stimulated the realization that I was dreaming! In the light of my lucid consciousness, the already impressive splendor of the castle appeared even more marvelously vibrant, and with great excitement I began to explore the imaginary reality of my "castle in the air." Walking down the hall, I could feel the cold hardness of the stones beneath my feet and hear the echo of my steps. Every element of this enchanting spectacle seemed "as real as real could be"—in spite of the fact that I remained perfectly aware that it was all a dream!

Fantastic as it may sound, while dreaming and soundly asleep, I was in full possession of my waking faculties: I could think as clearly as ever, freely remember details of my waking life, and act deliberately upon conscious reflection. Yet, none of this diminished the vividness of my dream; paradox or no, I was awake in my dream!

Finding myself before two diverging passageways, I exercised my free will, choosing to take the rightward one and shortly came upon a stairway. Curious about where it might lead, I descended the flight of steps and found myself near the top of an enormous subterranean vault. From where I stood at the foot of the stairs, the floor of the cavern sloped steeply downward, fading in the distance into darkness. Several hundred yards below I could see what appeared to be a fountain surrounded by marble statuary.

The idea of bathing in the symbolically renewing waters of the spring captured my fancy, and I proceeded at once down the hillside. Not on foot, however, for whenever I want to get somewhere in these dreams, I fly. As soon as I alighted beside the pool, I was at once startled by the discovery that what from above had seemed merely an inanimate statue now appeared unmistakably and ominously alive. Towering above the fountain stood a huge and intimidating genie, the Guardian of the Spring, as I somehow immediately knew. All my instincts cried out, "Flee!" But I remembered that this terrifying sight was only a dream; emboldened by this thought, I cast aside fear and flew straight up to the apparition.

As is the way of dreams, as soon as we were within reach, we had somehow become of equal size and I was able to look him in the eyes, face to face. Resolving to overcome my fear, I took both his hands in mine. As the dream slowly faded, the genie's power seemed to flow into me and I awoke, filled with vibrant energy. I felt like I was ready for anything.

—S.L., Palo Alto, California[1]

Strange, marvelous, and even impossible things regularly happen in dreams, but people usually do not realize that the explanation is that they are dreaming. *Usually* does not mean *always* and there is a highly significant exception to this generalization. Sometimes, dreamers *do* correctly realize the explanation for the bizarre happenings they are experiencing, and *lucid dreams*, like those recounted above, are the result.

Empowered by the knowledge that the world they are experiencing is a creation of their own imagination, lucid dreamers can consciously influence the outcome of their dreams. They can create and transform objects, people, situations, worlds, and even themselves. By the standards of the familiar world of physical and social reality, they can do the impossible.

The world of lucid dreams provides a vaster stage than ordinary life for almost anything imaginable, from the frivolous to the sublime. You could, if you chose, revel at a Saturnalian festival, soar to the stars, or travel to mysterious lands. You could join those who are testing lucid dreaming as a tool for problem solving, self-healing, and personal growth. Or you could explore the implications of teachings from ancient traditions and reports from modern psychologists that suggest that lucid dreams can help you find your deepest identity—who you really are.

Lucid dreaming has been known about for centuries, but has until recently remained a rare and little-understood phenomenon. My own scientific and personal explorations, together with the findings of other dream researchers around the world, have just begun to shed light on this unusual state of consciousness. Recently, this new research field has captured the attention of the population outside the world of scientific dream research because studies have shown that, given proper training, people can learn to have lucid dreams.

But why are people interested in learning to be conscious in their dreams? According to my own experience and the testimony of thousands of other lucid dreamers, lucid dreams can be extraordinarily vivid, intense, pleasurable, and exhilarating. People frequently consider their lucid dreams as among the most wonderful experiences of their lives.

If this were all there was to it, lucid dreams would be delightful, but ultimately trivial, entertainment. However, as many have already discovered, you can use lucid dreaming to improve the quality and depth of your life.

You can learn from your dream experiences just as much as from your waking life experiences. Chapter 5, *Lucid Dream Work: From Nightmares to Wholeness*, will focus on learning how to use your lucid dreams for self-integration and personal growth, as one of my own dreams illustrates:

I was in the middle of a riot in a classroom: a violent mob of thirty or forty was taking the place apart, throwing chairs and people through windows, grappling convulsively with each other and letting fly random shrieks, war cries, and insults— in short, the sort of thing that is likely to happen in certain grade schools when the teacher steps out of the classroom for a moment. The Goliath and leader of the Huns, a huge, repulsive barbarian with a pockmarked face, had locked me in an ironclad grip, and I was desperately struggling to get away. Then I realized that I was dreaming, and in a flash, I remembered the lessons of past experience.

I stopped struggling, for I knew that the conflict was with myself. I reasoned that the barbarian was a dream personification of something I was struggling with in myself. Or perhaps it represented someone, or some quality in another, that I disliked. In any case, this barbarian was obviously a Shadow figure if I had ever seen one! Experience had shown me that in the dream world, if nowhere else, the best way to bring hate and conflict to an end was to love my enemies as myself. What I needed to do, I realized, was to completely accept with open arms the Shadow I had been attempting to disown.

So, I tried to feel loving as I stood face to face with the Shadow Hun. I failed at first, feeling only repulsion and disgust. My gut reaction was that he was simply too ugly and barbarous to love. Determined to overcome the initial shock of the image, I sought love within my heart. Finding it, I looked the barbarian in the eyes, trusting my intuition to supply the right things to say. Beautiful words of acceptance flowed out of me, and as they did, my Shadow melted into me. The riot had vanished without a trace, the dream faded, and I awoke feeling wonderfully calm.

Although the outlines of a practical art and science of lucid dreaming are just beginning to emerge, and the systematic use of lucid dreaming as a tool for psychological self-exploration is still in its infancy, most people can safely use the available knowledge about lucid dreaming to conduct their own explorations. Probably the only people who should *not* experiment with lucid dreaming are those who are unable to distinguish between waking reality and constructions of their imagination. Learning lucid dreaming will not cause you to lose touch with the difference between waking and dreaming. On the contrary, lucid dreaming is for becoming *more aware.*

LIFE IS SHORT

Before we get into the specifics of how to have lucid dreams, let us take a closer look at the reasons for learning to awaken in your dreams. Do the potential benefits justify the costs in terms of the time and effort required for mastering lucid dreaming? We think so, but read on, and decide for yourself.

Proverbially and undeniably, life is short. To make matters worse, we must spend between a quarter and a half of our lives asleep. Most of us are in the habit of virtually sleepwalking through our dreams. We sleep, mindlessly, through many thousands of opportunities to be fully aware and alive.

Is sleeping through your dreams the best use of your limited lifespan? Not only are you wasting part of your finite store of time to be alive, but you are also missing adventures and lessons that could enrich the rest of your life. By awakening to your dreams, you will add to your experience of life and, if you use these added hours of lucidity to experiment and exercise your mind, you can also improve your enjoyment of your waking hours.

"Dreams are a reservoir of knowledge and experience," writes Tarthang Tulku, a Tibetan Buddhist lama teaching in Berkeley, "yet they are often overlooked as a vehicle for exploring reality. In the dream state our bodies are at rest, yet we see and hear, move about, and are even able to learn. When we make good use of the dream state, it is almost as if our lives were doubled: instead of a hundred years, we live two hundred."[2]

We can carry not only knowledge but also moods from the lucid dream state to the waking state. When we awaken laughing with delight from a wonderful lucid dream, it is not surprising to find that our waking mood has been brightened with feelings of joy. A young woman's first lucid dream, which she had after reading an article about lucid dreaming, provides a vivid example. Upon realizing she was dreaming, she "tried to remember the advice in the article," but the only thing that came to mind was a notion of her own: "ultimate experience." She felt herself taken over by a "blissful sensation of blending and melting with colors and light" that continued, "opening up into a total 'orgasm.'" Afterward, she "gently floated into waking consciousness" and was left with "a feeling of bubbling joy" that persisted for a week or more.[3]

This carry-over of positive feeling into the waking state is an important aspect of lucid dreaming. Dreams, remembered or not, often color our mood upon awakening, sometimes for a good part of a day. Just as the negative aftereffect of "bad dreams" can cause you to feel as if you got up on the wrong side of the bed, the positive feelings of a pleasant dream can give you an emotional uplift, helping you to start the day with confidence and energy. This is all the more true of inspirational lucid dreams.

Perhaps you are still thinking, "My dream life is interesting enough as it is. Why should I make an effort to enhance my awareness of it?" If so, consider the traditional mystical teaching that holds that most of humanity is asleep. When Idries Shah, the preeminent Sufi teacher, was asked to name "a fundamental mistake of man's," he replied, "to think that he is alive, when he has merely fallen asleep in life's waiting room."[4]

Lucid dreaming can help us understand Shah's words. Once you have had the experience of realizing that you are dreaming and that your possibilities are far greater than you had thought, you can imagine what a similar realization would be like in your waking life. As Henry David Thoreau put it, "Our truest life is when we are in dreams awake."

. . .
LISTEN TO TRACK 1
Your Present State of
Consciousness and the
Lucid Dream State
. . .

LUCID DREAMING AND WAKING LIFE

How does your renewed appreciation of the richness of your ordinary waking state of consciousness relate to the experience of lucid dreaming? Much of what you just observed about your present experiential world applies as well to the dream world. If you were dreaming, you would experience a multisensory world as rich and apparently real as the world you are experiencing right now. You would see, hear, feel, taste, think, and *be* just as you are now.

The crucial difference is that the multisensory world you experience while dreaming originates *internally* rather than *externally*. While awake, most of what you perceive corresponds to actually existing people, objects, and events in the external world. Because the objects of waking perception actually exist independently of your mind, they remain relatively stable. For example, you can look at this sentence, shut the book for a moment, and reopen to the same page, and you will see the same sentence.

But, as you will see in Chapter Two, the same is not true for dreaming. Because there is no stable external source of stimulation from which to build your experiential world, dreams are much more changeable than the physical world.

If you were in a lucid dream, your experience of the world would be even more different from waking life. First of all, you would know it was all a dream. Because of this, the world around you would tend to rearrange and transform even more than is usual in dreams. Impossible things could happen, and the dream scene itself, rather than disappearing once you know it to be "unreal," might increase in clarity and brilliance until you found yourself dumbfounded with wonder.

If *fully* lucid, you would realize that the entire dream world was in your own mind, and with this awareness might come an exhilarating feeling of freedom. Nothing external, no laws of society or physics, would constrain your experience; you could do anything you could conceive of, anything you believed you could do. Thus inspired, you might fly to the heavens. You might face a situation that you have been fearfully avoiding; you might enjoy an erotic encounter that surpasses what you had previously imagined, or experience symbolic union with your inner opposite; you might discover what it would be like to visit once more a loved one who has passed beyond the world of the living; you might seek and find a measure of self-knowledge and wisdom.

By cultivating awareness of and in your dreams and learning to use your magic carpet, you can add more consciousness, more life to your life. In the process, you will increase your enjoyment of your nightly dream journeys and deepen your understanding of yourself. By waking in your dreams, you can waken to life.

2

A Psychobiological
Model of Dreaming

. . .

The brain is wider than the sky,
For, put them side by side,
The one the other will contain
With ease, and you beside.
—EMILY DICKINSON

If this [a scientific finding] contradicts some aspect of Buddhist doctrine
as contained in the scriptures, we have no other choice but to accept
that that teaching is in need of interpretation. Thus, we cannot accept
it literally simply because it has been taught by the Buddha; we have
to examine whether it is contradicted by reason or not. If it does not
stand up to reason, we cannot accept it literally. We have to analyze
such teachings to discover the intention and purpose behind them
and regard them as subject to interpretation. Therefore, in Buddhism
great emphasis is laid on the importance of investigation.
—HIS HOLINESS THE DALAI LAMA XIV[1]

. . .

Proverbially, dreamers tend to have their heads in the clouds. Thus it is all too
easy for them to lose their orientation. The scientific approach of this chapter
provides a salutary grounding. Especially for those prospective explorers of the
dream world ("oneironauts") who think they are not interested in science, this
chapter should be considered required reading.

WHAT IS A DREAM?

Every night we enter another world, the world of dreams. While we are dreaming, we usually implicitly believe that we are awake. The mental worlds of dreams are so convincingly real that we mistake them for the outside world that we share with other people. How can this be? Why does it happen? What is the relation between our day and night lives? And what is the origin and function of dreaming? Incredibly, in this age of scientific understanding of the most intricate workings of biology, there is little scientific consensus about the answers to these questions.

The Oxford English Dictionary defines a dream as "a train of thoughts, images, or fancies passing through the mind during sleep."[2] But such a definition fails to capture the lived-in, experiential reality of dreams. In my view, dreams are much more accurately described as experiences—that is, conscious events one has personally encountered. It may seem odd to speak of dreams as conscious experiences, but the essential criterion for consciousness is reportability, and the fact that we can sometimes remember our dreams shows them to be conscious rather than unconscious mental processes. We live through our dreams as much as our waking lives. In these terms, dreaming is a particular organization of consciousness.

Of course, that begs a question: what is consciousness? For me, it is the dream of what happens. Whether awake or asleep, your consciousness functions as a simplified model of yourself and your world constructed by your brain from the best available sources of information. During waking, the model is derived from external sensory input, which provides the most current information about present circumstances, in combination with internal contextual, historical, and motivational information. During sleep, little external input is available, and given a sufficiently functional brain, the model is constructed from internal biases. These will be expectations derived from past experience and motivations—wishes, for example, as Sigmund Freud observed, but also fears. The resulting experiences are what we call dreams, the content of which is largely determined by what we fear, hope for, and expect. From this perspective, dreaming can be viewed as the special case of perception without the constraints of external sensory input. Conversely, perception can be viewed as the special case of dreaming constrained by sensory input.

There are two kinds of sleep. The first is an energy-conserving state known as Quiet Sleep (QS) associated with growth, repair, restoration, a relaxed body, and an idling brain. The second is a very different state known variously as Active Sleep, Paradoxical Sleep (PS), or REM. This state is associated with rapid eye movements and muscular twitches, a paralyzed body, a highly activated brain, and dreaming. Although REM is not the only sleep state in which people can dream, it provides the optimal conditions for vivid dreaming—a switched-on brain in a switched-off body.

DREAMING AND WAKING SIMILARITIES AND DIFFERENCES

It is frequently assumed that waking and dreaming experiences are completely distinct. Dreams, for example, are said to be characterized by lack of reflection, lack of control over attention, and the inability to act deliberately. But the evidence flatly contradicts this characterization of dreams as single-minded and nonreflective. In recent studies directly comparing reports from waking and dreaming, my colleagues Tracy Kahan, Lynne Levitan, Philip Zimbardo, and I found that, compared to waking experiences, dreaming contained public self-consciousness and emotion slightly more frequently, and deliberate choice slightly less frequently. However, no significant differences between dreaming and waking was found for other cognitive activities, and none of the measured cognitive functions was typically absent or rare in dreams. In particular, nearly identical levels of reflection were reported in both states.

The fact that dreams contain sudden shifts of characters and scenes of which the dreamer takes little note is sometimes cited as evidence for a cognitive deficiency in dreaming. The presumption is that if this occurred in waking, one would immediately notice and attempt to understand the discontinuity. However, this assumption is unwarranted. Recent studies on "change blindness" have shown that people are far less likely to detect environmental changes than common sense assumes. For example, in a recently completed study with Philip Zimbardo at Stanford, we showed twenty-eight college students a fifty-minute selection from Luis Buñuel's film *That Obscure Object of Desire*. Only seven of the subjects (twenty-five percent) noticed that the eponymous character of the title was played by two different actresses in alternating scenes—and the two did not even look similar.

I am not saying that there are no differences between dreams and waking experiences, because indeed there are distinctions. For example, the dream world is much less stable than the waking world because a dream lacks the stabilization of an external structure—physical reality. Likewise, one can violate the laws of physics and society in dreams without the usual consequences. But the absence of sensory constraint is the only essential difference. One might or might not know that one is dreaming, and the dream would still be a dream. And whatever differences there may be between the two, I believe they are more alike than they are different. As the early twentieth-century English physician and writer Havelock Ellis said, "Dreams are real while they last. Can we say more of life?"

EVOLUTION OF SLEEP AND DREAMS

It is likely that REM evolved for purposes more basic than dreaming. Just as philosophy, poetry, music, and abstract mathematics are probably the lucky side effects of other features that emerged through natural selection—such as general-purpose language—so dreaming is perhaps something that humans do, and extract value from, but that did not evolve directly.

The distribution of REM across development and in the course of a night provides a clue to the most important functions of this sleeping state. REM is at its maximal level perinatally and in the last weeks of prenatal development when the brain is growing its vast networks of neural circuitry. The appealing idea that REM serves as an endogenous ("self-organizing") state for the unfolding of genetic programming has been proposed by several researchers, including French sleep researcher Michel Jouvet and Stanford University psychiatrist William C. Dement. The percentage of REM activity gradually drops off throughout childhood but does not completely disappear when brain growth stops at adulthood, implying that REM may serve another function. The fact that REM gradually increases through the night, reaching a maximum as the time of wakening approaches, suggests that it may prepare our brains for waking action—a sort of brain tune-up. These recurrent activations every ninety minutes or so throughout the night may also help consolidate new learning.

WHY DREAMS ARE DIFFICULT TO RECALL

The average person remembers a dream only once or twice a week. Given the fact that we all dream every night, that leaves at least ninety-five percent of most dreams forgotten (in REM alone, assuming five REM cycles per night with perhaps two dreams per each REM period). A variety of theories have suggested fanciful explanations as to why dreams are so easily forgotten, ranging from Freud's belief that dreams are repressed because they contain so much taboo dream thought, to Francis Crick's view that the content of dreams is what the brain is trying to unlearn and therefore ought not to be remembered. Of course, standard memory theory explains much of what is remembered of dreams and what is not, which aspects of dream content are more readily recalled and which aspects are not, and so on. But these explanations do not answer the basic question of why it should be that dreams are so difficult to remember.

The answer, as I have proposed elsewhere, is probably evolution. Humans learn that dreams are distinct from other experiences by talking with other humans. Nonspeaking animals, however, have no way to tell each other how to distinguish dreams from reality. Thus, explicit dream recall would have been maladaptive for all the nonlinguistic mammals experiencing REM sleep during the past 140 million years since REM evolved. The purpose of REM cannot therefore have anything to do with the explicit recall of dreams, to say nothing of dream interpretation! To make the argument concrete, let us suppose you had a mutant cat that remembered its dreams. Suppose we say it lives on the other side of a tall fence that protects it from a vicious dog. Suppose further that your cat dreams that the wicked dog was dead, and replaced by a family of tasty mice. What would happen if the cat were to remember this dream when it awoke? Not knowing it was a dream, it would probably hungrily jump over the fence, expecting to find a meal. After its encounter with the dog, it would be less likely to pass on genes for easy dream recall.

Thus explicit dream recall obviously is maladaptive for cats, dogs, bats, whales, and all of the rest of the mammalian dreamers except humans. This fact very likely explains why dreams are difficult to recall. They may be so, according to this view, because of natural selection. We and our ancestors might have been protected from dangerous confusion by the evolution of mechanisms that made forgetting dreams the normal course of affairs. But if this theory is correct, since humans *can* tell the difference between dreams and waking reality, remembering dreams should do us no harm, and indeed may inspire us to remake reality in accord with our dreams.

Even if dreaming has no special biological function, dreams themselves may play a specific role. They may, for example, increase variability in the nervous system. Darwinian evolution requires a variable population, a selective pressure, and a means of reproduction of successful variations. Perhaps dreaming generates a wide range of behavioral schemas or scripts guiding perception and action from which to select adaptive responses to changing environments. Be that as it may, answers about why we dream need not be framed so narrowly. For some, the answer is: we dream to find out why we dream. Personally, I prefer: I dream to find out who I am beyond who I dream I am.

The view of dreams as world models is far from the traditional notion of dreams as messages, whether from the gods or from the unconscious mind. Nonetheless, interpretation of dreams can be very revealing of personality and a rewarding practice. If what people see in inkblots can tell something about their personal concerns and personality, how much more revealing should dreams be, because they are the worlds we have created from the contents of our minds. Dreams are not intended as messages, but they are our own most intimately personal creations. As such, they are revealingly colored by who and what we are, and who and what we could become.

SCIENTIFIC EVIDENCE FOR LUCID DREAMING

Our dreams seem so real that it is usually only when we wake up that we recognize them as the mental experiences they are. Although this is how we generally experience dreams, there is a significant exception: sometimes while dreaming, we consciously notice that we are dreaming. This clear-sighted state of consciousness is referred to as lucid dreaming.

During lucid dreams, one can reason clearly, remember the conditions of waking life, and act voluntarily within the dream upon reflection or in accordance with plans decided upon before sleep—all while remaining soundly asleep, vividly experiencing a dream world that can appear astonishingly real.

Until recently, researchers doubted that the dreaming brain was capable of such a high degree of mental functioning and consciousness. In the late 1970s, our laboratory research at Stanford University proved that lucid dreams did in fact occur during unambiguous sleep. Based on earlier studies showing that some of the eye movements of REM corresponded to the reported direction of the dreamer's gaze, we asked lucid dreamers to carry out distinctive patterns of voluntary eye movements when they realized they were dreaming. The prearranged eye-movement signals appeared on the polygraph records during uninterrupted REM, proving that the subjects had indeed been lucid during sleep.

Subsequently, my colleagues and I began new studies of the dreaming mind, made possible by the ability of lucid dreamers to carry out experiments within dreams. We learned that the physiological effects on the brain and body of dream activities are nearly identical to the effects of experience in waking life. For example, we found that time intervals estimated in lucid dreams closely match actual clock time, that dreamed breathing corresponds to actual respiration, that dreamed movements result in corresponding patterns of muscle twitching, and that dream sex shows physiological responses similar to actual sexual activity.

These studies all support the following picture: During REM dreaming, the events we consciously experience (or seem to) are the results of patterns of neural activity that, in turn, produce effects on our bodies. While to some extent these effects are modified by the specific conditions of active sleep, they remain virtually equivalent to the effects that would occur if we were actually to experience the corresponding events while awake. This explains, in part, why we regularly mistake our dreams for reality: to the functional systems of neuronal activity that construct the experiential world model of our consciousness, dreaming of perceiving or doing something is equivalent to actually perceiving or doing it.

3

Learning Lucid Dreaming

Methods for Developing the Skill
of Lucid Dreaming

· · ·

The vast majority of people have enormous potentialities of thinking,
far beyond anything ordinarily suspected; but so seldom do the right
circumstances by chance surround them to require their actualization that the
vast majority die without realizing more than a fraction of their powers. Born
millionaires, they live and die in poverty for the lack of favorable circumstances
which would have compelled them to convert their credit into cash.
—A. R. ORAGE, *PSYCHOLOGICAL EXERCISES AND ESSAYS*[1]

· · ·

LEARNING TO DREAM

Just as we ordinarily take for granted that we know how to think, we may also
presume that we know how to dream. But there are vast differences in the degree
to which these two faculties are developed in different people. Orage's remarks
about thinking apply, I believe, with equal force to dreaming. We possess unde-
veloped capacities yet undreamed of. Like conscious thought, lucid dreaming is
an ability that can be gained or improved by training, and this chapter will show
you how to practice.

In my view there are three essential requirements for learning lucid dreaming:
adequate motivation, correct practice of effective techniques, and excellent dream
recall. The necessity of motivation is obvious enough: lucid dreaming, after all,
demands considerable control of attention, and hence you must be motivated to
exert the necessary effort to focus your mind and intention. But the amount of

motivation required is not extremely high. Having a lucid dream does not have to be the most important thing in the world for you to succeed in inducing one. But it does have to be something that you genuinely want to, and more importantly, *expect* to happen.

The necessity of correct practice of effective techniques is easily seen: even if you have all the motivation in the world to learn to, say, play the piano, you will not be able to do it if you keep your fingers in your ears, or if you believe you can learn to play by sleeping with a piano book under your pillow.

There are several reasons why developing excellent dream recall is an essential prerequisite for learning lucid dreaming. First, when you remember your dreams well, you can become familiar with what they are actually like. Once you get to know your dreams really well, you will be in the position of recognizing them as dreams *while* they are still happening. Second, it is possible that with poor dream recall, you may actually have lucid dreams that you do not remember! Finally, as you will soon see, the most effective lucid dream induction method—the Mnemonic Induction of Lucid Dreams (MILD) technique—requires you to remember more than one dream per night. Hence, for the purposes of learning lucid dreaming, excellent dream recall means remembering at least one dream per night. To put that in perspective, the average person remembers only a few dreams per week, and we all have at least half a dozen dreams per night.

DEVELOPING EXCELLENT DREAM RECALL

Getting plenty of sleep is the first step toward good dream recall. If you are rested, it will be easier to focus on your goal of recalling dreams, and you will not mind so much taking the time during the night to record your dreams. Another benefit of getting plenty of sleep is that dream periods get longer and closer together as the night proceeds. The first dream of the night is the shortest, perhaps only five to ten minutes long, while after eight hours of sleep, dream periods can last forty to sixty minutes. We all dream every night, about one dream period every ninety minutes. People who say they never dream simply never remember their dreams.

You may have more than one dream during a REM (dream) period, separated by short arousals that are most often forgotten.

It can be useful while you are developing your dream recall to keep a complete dream journal. Keep the journal handy by your bed and record every dream you remember, no matter how fragmentary. Start by writing down all your dreams, not just the complete, coherent, or interesting ones—even if all you remember is a face or a room, write it down.

When you awaken in the night and recall what you were dreaming, record the dream right away. If you do not, in the morning you may find you remember nothing about the dream, and you will certainly have forgotten many interesting details. If you do not feel like writing out a long dream story in the middle of the night, you can memorize the dream and just note the key points of the plot. You can then use your notes to write out the full dream in the morning.

Possibly, all you will need to do to increase your dream recall is to remind yourself as you are falling asleep that you wish to awaken fully from your dreams and remember them. This works in a similar manner to remembering to awaken at a certain time in the morning. While you are at it, why not tell yourself you will have interesting, meaningful, and lucid dreams?

A major cause of forgetting dreams is interference from other mental content (i.e., thoughts, feelings, events, etc.) competing for your attention. Therefore, try to let your first thought upon awakening be, "What was I just dreaming?" Before attempting to write down the dream, go over the dream in your mind, retelling the dream story to yourself until you remember it as a whole.

Important! For optimal dream recall, do not move from the position in which you awaken. Hold completely still, and focus your attention only on what was just going through your mind. Avoid the usual pattern of thinking of the day's concerns immediately upon awakening. Scan for any clues of what you might have been experiencing—moods, feelings, fragments of images, or thoughts. Ask yourself, "Now why was I thinking *that?*" and you will frequently find that you were not just thinking whatever, but *dreaming*. When you recall a scene, try to recall what happened before that, and before that, and so on, reliving the dream in reverse.

If you find that you sleep straight through the night without being conscious of waking from your dreams, you might try drinking a little coffee, tea, or other caffeinated beverage before bed—not enough to keep you awake, but enough to get you out of bed during the night. You can also try setting an alarm clock to wake you at a time when you are likely to be dreaming. Since REM periods occur at approximately ninety-minute intervals, good times will be close to multiples of ninety minutes after you go to sleep. Aim for the later REM periods by setting the alarm for four and a half, six, or seven and a half hours after you go to sleep. Once again, when you wake up, do not move. Instead, think first of what you were just dreaming before writing.

To remind yourself of your intentions and get yourself into the spirit of your dreams, read through your dream journal at bedtime. Learning to remember your dreams may take particular effort at first, but if you persist, you will almost certainly succeed—and may find yourself effortlessly remembering four or more dreams per night. Of course, once you reach this level, you probably will not want to write them all down—just the significant or compelling ones. The more familiar you become with the style of your own dreams, the easier it will be to remember you are dreaming while you are dreaming—and explore the world of your dreams while still on the scene.

WAKING UP IN THE DREAM
Getting to Know Your "Dreamsigns"

In the more common of the two ways that people experience lucid dreams, the dreamer somehow realizes that he or she is dreaming while in the midst of an ongoing dream in uninterrupted REM sleep. This is termed a Dream Initiated Lucid Dream, or DILD.

So let us suppose that you now have excellent dream recall. This means that on most nights you vividly recall at least one of your dreams, and if you wish, it is easy to recall two or three or more. Now you can start to get to know what makes your dreams dreamlike. As we discussed in Chapter Two, dreams and waking experiences are more alike than different, and much of what happens during your night life will be little different from what happens during your day life. But for the purposes of developing lucid dreaming, you need to focus on the differences—the ways in which dream experiences differ from waking life experiences. Those aspects of dream content that reliably differ from the corresponding experiences of waking life, and hence can clue in the attentive dreamer to the fact that he or she is at that moment dreaming, are referred to as "dreamsigns."

I coined this term twenty years ago to conveniently refer to all those elements of dreams that can indicate that you are dreaming. Examples, taken at random, might include miraculous flight, irrational thinking or anomalous emotional response (either too strong or too weak for the context), malfunctioning devices, meeting deceased people or celebrities, etc. By studying your dreams, you can become familiar with your personal dreamsigns and resolve to recognize them as such the next time you see them and thereby become lucid in future dreams.

There are two distinct classes of dreamsign. "Strong dreamsigns" are necessary and sufficient conditions for concluding that one is dreaming—that is, events that can happen *only* in dreams (e.g., impossibilities like walking on water or levitating). "Weak dreamsigns" indicate events that are merely improbable in waking life but characteristic of dreams, such as meeting celebrities, finding money in the street, etc. The basic strategy of using dreamsign awareness to induce lucid dreaming is to firmly resolve to (i.e., set your intention to) recognize any dreamsign noticed in the future for what it is, and thus become lucid.

The late Paul Tholey, a German psychologist and world-class oneironaut, developed and tested a variety of techniques for inducing lucid dreams, derived from over a decade of research involving more than 200 subjects. According to Dr. Tholey, the most effective method of learning to achieve lucidity is to develop "a critical-reflective attitude" toward your state of consciousness by asking yourself whether or not you are dreaming while you are awake. Tholey stressed the importance of asking "the critical question"—"Am I dreaming or not?"—as frequently as possible (at least five to ten times a day) and in every situation that seems dreamlike. That is, at any appearance of a dreamsign, weak or strong. Asking the question at bedtime and while falling asleep is also favorable.

Following this technique, most people will have their first lucid dream within a month, Tholey reports, and some will succeed on the very first night.

...
LISTEN TO TRACK 2
Guided Reality Test
...
The following is modified from Tholey's combined reflection-intention technique. The accompanying audio includes a very similar technique: the Guided Reality Test.

COMBINED REALITY TEST WITH INTENTION SETTING

1 **Do a reality test.** Carry some text with you or wear a digital watch throughout the day. To do a reality test, read the words or the numbers on the watch. Then, look away and look back, observing the letters or numbers to see if they change. Try to make them change while watching them. Our research shows that in lucid dreams, text changes seventy-five percent of the time it is reread once and changes ninety-five percent of the time it is reread twice. If the characters do change, are not normal, or do not make sense, then you are most probably dreaming. Enjoy! If the characters are normal, stable, and sensible, then you probably are not dreaming. Go on to step 2.

2 **Imagine that your surroundings are a dream**. If you are fairly certain you are awake (you can never be completely certain!), then tell yourself, "I may not be dreaming now, but if I were, what would it be like?" Visualize as vividly as possible that you are dreaming. Intently imagine that what you are seeing, hearing, smelling, and feeling is all a dream. Imagine instabilities in your environment, words changing, scenes transforming, perhaps you are floating off the ground. Create in yourself the feeling that you are in a dream. Holding that feeling, continue with step 3.

3 **Visualize yourself enjoying a dream activity.** Decide (in advance) on something you would like to do in your next lucid dream, perhaps flying, talking to particular dream characters, or just exploring the dream world. Continue to imagine that you are dreaming now, and visualize yourself enjoying your chosen activity.

4 **Firmly resolve to be lucid and to carry out your chosen activity.** While continuing to imagine yourself doing what you want to do in your next lucid dream, tell yourself firmly: "Next time I'm dreaming I want to recognize I'm dreaming and to do whatever I want to do in that lucid dream." Repeat the resolution several times until you feel your intention is firmly set.

Using Missed Dreamsigns as Stepping Stones to Lucidity

Most of the dreams you recall will contain at least one but more likely several dreamsigns. Until you have developed at least a moderate degree of lucidity, you will almost never recognize these dream oddities for what they are, and this leads to a pitfall which can block progress until it is understood and corrected: the mistake (common among novice lucid dreamers) is to focus on how uncritical their minds are during dreaming, using each missed dreamsign as another example proving that they *never* recognize dreamsigns. This is a mistake! If you do this, you use missed dreamsigns to learn that you are too unreflective, stupid, or simply lacking in the capability to become lucid. This is not what you want to learn, is it?

What you do want to learn is how to recognize when you are dreaming by getting to know your dreamsigns. Thus you should make sure that you reflect on which parts of your dream could have told you that you were dreaming, and resolve that the *next time* something like that dreamsign reoccurs, you *will* remember that you are dreaming! So, if you awake from a dream in which you failed to notice that the friend you were talking to has been dead for years, you must *firmly* resolve that if you ever see that person again, you will realize that you are dreaming. Furthermore, resolve that you *will* see your friend again, and that the *next time* you do, you *will* become lucid.

Missed dreamsigns are like stepping stones across Lethe, the river of forgetfulness, to the promised "Lucidland," but only if you use them as such, only if you decide with complete conviction that you won't get fooled again. Of course, you will. To err is human, but why not learn to err less and less?

REMEMBERING THE FUTURE:
MNEMONIC INDUCTION OF LUCID DREAMS

It's a poor sort of memory that only works backwards.

—Lewis Carroll, *Alice in Wonderland*

The most powerful technique for inducing lucid dreams is based upon "prospective memory," remembering to do something (i.e., notice that you are dreaming) in the future. While most of what you think of as memory involves retrieving information from the past, prospective memory, or memory for intentions, refers to our ability to remember our intention to carry out some specific action at a future time or circumstance.

Aside from writing ourselves memos (a device of little use here for obvious reasons!) we do this by forming a mental connection between what we want to remember to do and the future circumstances in which we intend to do it. Making this connection is greatly facilitated by the mnemonic device (i.e., memory aid) of visualizing yourself doing what you intend to remember. It is also helpful to verbalize the intention, "When such-and-such happens, I want to remember to do so-and-so." For example, "When I pass the bank, I want to remember to draw out some cash."

I developed this technique as part of my doctoral dissertation project and used it to achieve lucid dreaming at will. The verbalization that I use myself to organize my intended effort is, "Next time I'm dreaming I want to remember to recognize I'm dreaming." The "when" and the "what" of the intended action must be clearly specified.

The proper time to practice MILD is after awakening from a dream, before returning directly to sleep, or following a longer period of full wakefulness, as detailed below. An important point is that in order to produce the desired effect, it is necessary to do more than just mindlessly recite the phrase. You must really intend to have a lucid dream. Here is the recommended procedure spelled out step by step.

...
LISTEN TO TRACK 3
Mnemonic Induction of
Lucid Dreams
...

MNEMONIC INDUCTION OF LUCID DREAMS EXERCISE

1 **Set up dream recall.** At bedtime, set your mind to awaken from and to remember dreams. When you awaken from a dream, recall it as completely as you can.

2 **Focus your intent.** While returning to sleep, concentrate single-mindedly on your intention to remember to recognize that you are dreaming. Tell yourself, "Next time I'm dreaming, I will remember I'm dreaming," repeatedly, like a mantra. Put real feeling into the words and focus on this idea alone. If you find yourself thinking about anything else, let it go and bring your mind back to your intention.

3 **See yourself becoming lucid.** As you continue to focus on your intention to remember to recognize the next time you are dreaming, imagine that you are back in the dream from which you just awakened. Imagine that this time you recognize that you are dreaming. Identify a dreamsign, and when you see it, say to yourself, "I'm dreaming!" and continue your fantasy. Imagine yourself carrying out your plans for your next lucid dream. For example, if you want to fly in your lucid dream, imagine yourself flying.

4 **Repeat until your intention is set.** Repeat steps 2 and 3 until either you fall asleep you or are sure that your intention is set. If while falling asleep you find yourself thinking of anything else, repeat the procedure so that the last thing in your mind before falling asleep is your intention to remember to recognize the next time you are dreaming. If all goes well, in a short time you will find yourself lucid in another dream (which need not closely resemble the one you have rehearsed).

PHYSIOLOGICAL FACTORS INFLUENCING LUCID DREAMING

Lucid dreaming does not occur with equal frequency at all times. Lucid dreamers from Frederik van Eeden to Patricia Garfield have long reported that lucid dreams occur "almost exclusively" during the early morning hours. Our research at Stanford indicates that extended stable lucid dreams seem to occur exclusively during REM periods. Moreover, later REM periods are more conducive to lucidity than are earlier REM periods. Although it is certainly possible to induce lucid dreams during the first REM period of the night using MILD, it is much easier when practiced later in the sleep cycle, say after four and a half hours (REM period 3), or six hours (REM period 4).

If you find that you are just too drowsy to follow the procedure as described in the MILD Exercise, you might try to wake yourself up by engaging in several minutes of any activity that demands full wakefulness, such as writing down your dream, reading, or simply getting out of bed. This sleep interruption is itself a condition favoring lucidity.

In the late 1970s, I was led to develop sleep-interruption as a method of lucid dream induction after hearing a remarkably broad set of nocturnal activities that were claimed to be associated with immediately subsequent lucid dreaming. These included sex, vomiting, reading and writing, and pre-dawn meditation with a definite spirit of self-sacrifice. What did these putative lucidogenic activities have in common? The answer proved to be quite simple: wakefulness!

A period of wakefulness interrupting the normal course of sleep increases the likelihood of lucidity. In fact, the "morning nap" or "sleep interruption" technique, refined through several experiments conducted by the Lucidity Institute, is an extremely powerful method of stimulating lucid dreams. The technique simply requires you to wake from sleep one hour earlier than usual, stay awake for thirty to sixty minutes, then go back to sleep. One study showed a fifteen- to twenty-fold increased likelihood of lucid dreaming for thirty to sixty minutes of wakefulness compared to five minutes. During the sleep-interruption period, read about lucid dreaming, practice reality checks, and then practice MILD as you are falling asleep. The Lucidity Institute's training programs include this technique as an essential part of the schedule. It is one of the reasons why most participants have lucid dreams during the workshop.[1]

I said earlier in this chapter that I had been able to learn to have lucid dreams at will using a technique I developed over several years. That technique was, of course, MILD. Once I learned how to use it, I experienced as many as four lucid dreams in a single night, and indeed seemed able to attain lucidity on any night that I tried. I see no reason why the same could not be true for others as well.

Undoubtedly, the future will see the development of much more effective techniques for lucid dream induction that promise to make this world available to anyone who needs or desires it. Who knows? Perhaps entry into lucid dreams will one day be no more difficult than falling asleep.

WAKE INITIATED LUCID DREAMING (WILD)

This brings us to another class of lucid dream induction methods: falling asleep consciously. The second of the two main ways in which people become lucid is by briefly awakening from REM sleep and then returning right back to REM sleep without losing consciousness. This is termed a Wake Initiated Lucid Dream, or WILD. There are a number of techniques available for voluntarily inducing WILDs, all based on the same fundamental principle: you lie in bed, deeply relaxed but vigilant, and perform a repetitive or continuous mental activity upon which you focus your attention. Keeping this task going is what maintains your inner focus of attention and with it your wakeful inner consciousness, while your drowsy external awareness diminishes and finally vanishes altogether as you fall asleep. In essence, the idea is to let your body fall asleep while you keep your mind awake.

There are many variations on the technique of falling asleep while maintaining consciousness. Tarthang Tulku, a Tibetan lama teaching in Berkeley, describes a simple and effective method: after relaxing very deeply just before sleep, you visualize a beautiful lotus flower in your throat. In the center of this lotus is a red-orange flame. You gently focus your attention on the light of the flame as you fall asleep consciously. The accompanying audio includes a guided meditation on the Dream Lotus and Flame Technique.

...
LISTEN TO TRACK 4
Dream Lotus and
Flame Technique
...

PREVENTING PREMATURE AWAKENING

Beginning lucid dreamers often have the problem of waking up right after becoming lucid. This obstacle may prevent some people from realizing the value of lucid dreaming. Fortunately, there are ways to overcome this problem.

The first is to remain calm in the dream. Becoming lucid is exciting, but expressing the excitement too soon can awaken you. It is possible to enjoy the thrill that accompanies the dawning of lucidity without allowing the activation to overwhelm you. Be like a poker player with an ideal hand. Relax and engage with the dream rather than withdrawing into your inner joy of accomplishment.

Then, if the dream shows signs of ending, such as a loss of detail, vividness, or apparent reality of the imagery, the technique of "spinning" your dream body like a whirling dervish can often restore the imagery. I developed this technique serendipitously after having the (mistaken) idea that relaxing completely might help prevent awakening from lucid dreams. The next time I found myself in a fading lucid dream, I relaxed completely and dropped backward to the floor . . . and was disappointed to find myself back in bed. Or was I? After I actually awoke a minute later, I realized that I had had a "false awakening"—a partial success, in that dreaming continued. After a bit of testing, I determined that what stabilized the dream state was not relaxation but movement, or rather the sensation of motion. The best way to create a feeling of movement, especially if the dream scene has vanished, leaving nowhere to move to, is to spin like a top. You are not really spinning, but your brain is well familiar with the experience of spinning and duplicates the experience quite well. In the process, the vestibular and kinesthetic senses are engaged. Presumably, this sensory engagement with the dream inhibits the brain from changing state from dreaming to waking.

Be aware that the expectation of possible awakening sometimes leads to a false awakening in which you dream of waking. The vividness of the spinning sensation may cause you to feel your spinning arm hit the bed. You may think, "Oops, I'm awake in bed now." But be clear—it was not your physical body that was spinning, it was your dream body—therefore, the moving arm must be a dream arm hitting a dream bed! To avoid being deceived, continuously remind yourself while spinning, "The next thing I see will be a dream," until a scene appears. If you are in doubt about your status, perform a thorough reality test.

Research at the Lucidity Institute has proven the effectiveness of spinning: the odds in favor of continuing the lucid dream were better than twenty-to-one after spinning, compared to odds of only one-to-two after "going with the flow" (the control task). That makes the relative odds favoring spinning over going with the flow nearly fifty-to-one—well worth the minor investment of time to set your mind.

FUTURE ACCESS TO THE LUCID DREAM STATE

At present, it is possible to point to several techniques that could perhaps be profitably developed to induce lucid dreams. One is the use of hypnosis. "Auto-suggestion," or implanting in oneself the intention to do something, is a form of hypnosis; and it is involved in practicing MILD. Many people have found it at least moderately effective in inducing lucid dreams. Also, for the fortunate minority of the population who are easily hypnotizable, post-hypnotic suggestion to have lucid dreams may be more effective when given in a trance by a hypnotist, rather than when given by yourself. But even if you are not highly hypnotizable, you are fully able to benefit from positive suggestions and affirmations. The accompanying audio includes a Trance Induction of Lucid Dreaming in two versions, one for use in the daytime (Track 5) and one for use at bedtime (Track 6).

. . .

LISTEN TO TRACK 5
Trance Induction of
Lucid Dreaming: Day
and TRACK 6 Trance
Induction of Lucid
Dreaming: Night

. . .

LUCID DREAMING INDUCTION DEVICES (LDIDs)

The basis for most lucid dream induction procedures is to focus and reinforce your intention to remember to do something during your dream—namely, to recognize that you are dreaming. Wouldn't it be nice if while you were dreaming, someone could give you a reminder? As it happens, there are electronic devices available that can do just that. These lucid dream induction devices, or LDIDs, were developed in the course of our laboratory research at Stanford University. We found that flashing lights could be used as lucidity cues. Lights tended to be incorporated into ongoing dreams without causing awakening.

You may have noticed that occasional bits of sensory information are filtered into your dreams in disguised form, like a clock radio as supermarket music or a chain saw as the sound of a thunderstorm. This is the same principle used by LDIDs: the lights or sounds from the device filter into the user's dreams. The dreamer's task is to notice the flashing lights in the dream and remember that they are cues to become lucid.

The NovaDreamer® is a commercially available LDID consisting of a comfortable sleep mask equipped with infrared eye-movement sensors. When the sensors determine you are dreaming, the NovaDreamer delivers a lucidity cue in the form of flashing lights from a pair of bright red LEDs. The flashing light cues enter into ongoing dreams in a variety of ways. Cues can be superimposed over the dream scene, like a light flashing in one's face, or they can briefly interrupt the dream scene, or most commonly, they blend into the ongoing dream plot: little brother flashing the room lights, fireflies, lightning, traffic signals, police car lights, or flash cameras.

LDIDs do not *make* people have lucid dreams any more than exercise machines *make* people develop strong muscles. In both cases, the goal—lucid dreams or strength—results from *practice*. The machines simply accelerate the process. Scientific studies have verified that the current generation of LDIDs, correctly used, can effectively increase lucid dreaming frequency.

I believe that during the next decade or two we can look forward to increasingly effective LDIDs thanks to the rapid growth of computers and microelectronics. In case you fear that there is something wrong or unnatural about using technology to induce lucid dreaming, you will be interested to know that the Dalai Lama was delighted with the DreamLight® LDID (a close cousin of the NovaDreamer) when he saw it at a Mind and Life conference in 1997:

> This would be very good for practice while sleeping and dreaming. Sometimes, if you have a strong dream at night, when you wake up it affects your emotional state in the morning. With this we could cultivate wholesome states of mind while dreaming, and that would be of benefit. [2]

And to the benefits we now turn.

4

The Practical Dreamer
Applications of Lucid Dreaming

. . .

THE USE OF A NEWBORN BABY

Concerning electricity, a scientific curiosity of the eighteenth century, a woman is said to have asked Benjamin Franklin, "But what use is it?" His reply is famous: "What use, madame, is a newborn baby?" If 200 years later the same question were asked in regard to lucid dreaming, a scientific curiosity of the present century, the same answer could be given. Though we can only speculate at present, our work at Stanford and the accounts of other lucid dreamers suggests that, like electricity, lucid dreaming could also conceivably be harnessed to aid us in performing a variety of tasks with far greater ease.

Since the most general advantage offered by lucid consciousness to both dreaming and waking is the capacity for flexible and creative action, most of the various applications of lucid dreaming will themselves be examples of creativity, broadly defined.

Biofeedback researchers Elmer and Alyce Green have discussed creativity at three different levels of organization—physiological, psychological, and social. For example, in physiological processes, creativity means physical healing and regeneration. In emotional processes, creativity includes creating attitude changes which favor the establishment of inner harmony, and in the mental sphere it involves the synthesis of new ideas.

"The entrance, or key, to all these inner processes," the Greens were beginning to believe, was:

. . . a particular state of consciousness in which the gap between conscious and unconscious processes is voluntarily narrowed, and temporarily eliminated when useful. When that self-regulated reverie is established, the body can apparently be programmed at will, and the instructions given will be carried out, emotional states can be dispassionately examined, accepted or rejected, or totally supplanted by others deemed more useful, and problems insoluble in the normal state of consciousness can be elegantly resolved.[1]

I believe that what the Greens propose about the hypnagogic (or reverie) state applies all the more strongly to the lucid dreaming state, where the conscious mind encounters the unconscious, face to face.

THE HEALING DREAM

There have been times when I have fallen asleep in tears; but in my dreams the most charming forms have come to cheer me, and I have risen fresh and joyful.

—Goethe

The use of dreams for healing was widespread in the ancient world. The sick would sleep in the temples of Asklepios, the Greek god of healing; during their dreams, the god or his serpent familiar (hence the caduceus symbol of medicine) was said to appear, telling patients what they must do to be healed. Clearly we cannot evaluate either the effectiveness or mechanism of any resulting cures, but today we have reason to believe that dreams can indeed aid the healing process.

Health has been defined as "a state of optimal functioning with freedom from disease and abnormality."[2] The domain over which this functioning ranges is life in all its complexities. In general terms, health can be conceived of as a condition of adaptive responsiveness to the challenges of life. For responses to be adaptive, they must at least favorably resolve the situation in a way that does not disrupt the individual's integrity or wholeness. Adaptive responses also improve the individual's relationship with the environment. There are degrees of adaptiveness, with the optimum being what we have defined as health.

By this definition, being healthy involves more than simply maintaining the status quo. On the contrary, when our familiar behaviors are inadequate to cope with a situation, any healthy response will include learning new, hopefully more adaptive behaviors. When we learn new behaviors, we grow; having done so, we find ourselves better equipped to deal with the challenges of life.

Lucid dreaming bears a family resemblance to daydreaming, hypnagogic reverie, psychedelic drug states, hypnotic hallucinations, and other types of mental imagery. Since many members of the mental imagery family have found gainful employment in therapeutic circles, it would seem reasonable to expect that lucid dreaming might also prove effective here.

According to Drs. Dennis Jaffe and David Bresler, "Mental imagery mobilizes the latent, inner powers of the person, which have immense potential to aid in the healing process and in the promotion of health."[3] However it works, imagery is employed in a great variety of psychotherapeutic approaches ranging from psychoanalysis to behavior modification.

If, as appears likely, the efficacy of imagery is proportional to its experiential reality, it seems likely that healing imagery, occurring in the lucid dream state, should be especially effective—perhaps uniquely so. This is because dreaming is surely the most vivid form of imagery likely to be experienced by normal individuals. Thus what happens in lucid dreams has an understandably powerful impact on the dreamer, both experientially and physically.

Hypnosis is a therapeutic imagery technique that is probably relevant to lucid dreaming. Deeply hypnotized subjects are able to exert remarkable control over many of their physiological functions: inhibiting allergic reactions, stopping bleeding, and inducing anesthesia at will. Unfortunately, these dramatic responses seem to be limited to the five or ten percent of the population capable of entering hypnosis very deeply, and this capability does not appear to be trainable. In contrast, lucid dreaming is a learnable skill. Lucid dreams could hold the same potential for self-regulation as deep-trance hypnosis and be accessible to a much greater proportion of the population.

One of the most intriguing therapeutic applications of mental imagery is Dr. O. Carl Simonton's work with cancer patients. Dr. Simonton and his colleagues report that patients with advanced cancer who supplemented standard radiation and chemotherapy treatment with healing imagery survived on average twice as long as expected by national averages. While caution seems appropriate in interpreting these results, they still suggest some very exciting possibilities.

Given the fact that our laboratory studies have revealed a high correlation between dream behavior and physiological responses, it seems justifiable to hope that healing imagery during lucid dreaming might be even more effective. You could conceivably carry out actions in your lucid dreams specifically designed to accomplish whatever precise physiological consequences you desire. That leaves some fascinating possibilities for future research to explore: Can you initiate self-healing processes by consciously envisioning your dream body as perfectly healthy? If in lucid dreams you "heal" your dream body, to what extent will you also heal your physical body?

BENEFITS OF WORKING THROUGH FEARFUL DREAMS

He has not learned the lesson of life who does not every day surmount a fear.
—Ralph Waldo Emerson

Masakatsu agatsu. (True victory is mastery of self.)
—O Sensei

As I will discuss in detail in the next chapter, from my own experience I believe that facing and working through fearful dreams can be a valuable learning experience, providing an education in clarity and compassion that truly starts at home. At the beginning of my study of lucid dreaming, I noted that anxiety preceded lucidity onset in 36 percent of my first year's lucid dreams (60 percent during the first six months). In contrast, by the second year, anxiety was present when I recognized that I was dreaming in only about 19 percent of my lucid dreams. During the third year, anxiety appeared in only 5 percent, and in 1 percent or less during the following four years. I attribute the decrease in number and proportion of anxiety dreams to my practice of resolving conflicts during lucid dreams, in the manner I described earlier. This reduction seems especially impressive in light of the fact that my life has become much more stressful and demanding in the years since. If something were not resolving the stress of my daily life, I should be experiencing waking anxiety in recent years with concomitant increases in dream anxiety. However, I have been having less anxiety in my lucid dreams and perhaps also in waking life. It may therefore be the case that a lasting benefit of "responsible" lucid dreaming, of the sort I have been practicing, can result in more adaptive behaviors while asleep and perhaps while awake. Furthermore, as I explained earlier, I have learned to utilize anxiety itself as an infallible lucidity cue. In the last six years, I have not once been awakened from a dream by anxiety, as should have happened if I were having non-lucid nightmares. During this period, sufficient anxiety has always led to my awakening in my dream rather than from it, thereby affording me the opportunity to face my fears and resolve my conflicts.

This is a very important potential of lucid dreaming, for when we escape from a nightmare by awakening, we have not dealt with the problem of our fear or of our frightening dream, but have merely *temporarily* relieved the fear and repressed the fearful dream. Thus we are left with an unresolved conflict as well as, in all likelihood, negative and unhealthy feelings. On the other hand, staying with the nightmare and accepting its challenge, as lucidity makes possible, allows us to resolve the dream problem in a fashion that leaves us healthier than before. So if, as I have suggested, healing was the original intent of the dream that became the nightmare, lucidity can aid in the redemption of a dream gone wrong.

The flexibility and self-confidence that lucidity brings in its wake greatly enhances the dreamer's ability to master the situation presented by the dream. I believe the habit of flexibility to be well worth developing in the lucid dream. In addition to being highly effective in the dream world, it is also generally applicable in the waking world. Indeed, it may at times be the only course of action open to you. In most situations, it would be unrealistic to expect other people to change the way you may want them to. You cannot always or even often get others to do what you want; you may not even be able to prevent them from doing exactly what you do not want them to do. Nonetheless, at every moment, whether dreaming or waking, you have the power to reframe the way you see the circumstances in which you find yourself. You define your own experience: who and how you want to be, and how you choose to view the situation you face. In brief:

> Two men looked out prison bars;
> One saw mud, the other stars.
> > —Anonymous

Naturally, it is often not so obvious which outlook or course of action is best. Life often presents us with complex situations that require difficult decisions. As it happens, lucid dreaming may help us in choosing wisely.

CREATIVE PROBLEM SOLVING

Dreams have long been regarded as a wellspring of inspiration in nearly every field of human endeavor, from literature to science and engineering, from painting to music and sports. Space limits us to presenting only a few of the many available examples, but they should be enough to illustrate the role played by dreams in the creative process.

First, let us consider the case of the Russian chemist, Dmitri Mendeleev, who had been working for years in an effort to discover a way of classifying the elements according to their atomic weights. One night in 1869 the chemist fell into bed exhausted after devoting many long hours in an attempt to solve the problem. Later that night he "saw in a dream a table where all the elements fell into place as required." Upon awakening he immediately wrote down the table just as he remembered it on a piece of paper. Amazingly, Mendeleev reported, "Only in one place did a correction later seem necessary."[4] Thus the Periodic Table of the Elements, a fundamental discovery of modern physics, was first brought forth in a dream.

Jack Nicklaus provides a fascinating example of dream creativity. After winning a number of championships, the professional golfer found himself in an embarrassing slump. After he eventually regained his championship form seemingly overnight, a reporter asked him how he had done it. Nicklaus replied:

> I've been trying everything to find out what has been wrong. It was getting to the place where I figured a seventy-six was a pretty good round. But last Wednesday night I had a dream and it was about my golf swing. I was hitting them pretty good in the dream and all at once I realized I wasn't holding the club the way I've actually been holding it lately. I've been having trouble collapsing my right arm taking the club head away from the ball, but I was doing it perfectly in my sleep. So when I came to the course yesterday morning, I tried it the way I did in my dream and it worked. I shot a sixty-eight yesterday and a sixty-five today and believe me it's a lot more fun this way. I feel kind of foolish admitting it, but it really happened in a dream. All I had to do was change my grip just a little.[5]

I have seen similar examples of lucid dreams used for problem solving and improvement of performance in athletics, martial arts, and dance. One such report comes from a skater who lucid-dreamed a breakthrough in technique. Tanya writes that she had been a pretty good skater, but felt that something was holding her back. Then one night in a lucid dream, Tanya experienced "complete skating."

> In the dream I was in a rink with a number of other people. We were playing hockey and I was skating in the manner I always had, competent yet hesitant. At that moment I realized I was dreaming so I told myself to allow my higher knowledge to take over my consciousness. I surrendered to the quality of complete skating. Instantly there was no more fear, no more holding back and I was skating like a pro, feeling as free as a bird.

What we learn in lucid dreams usually applies to waking life in some way, and for motor skills, that usually means directly. Tanya reported successful generalization of her dream-learning:

> The next time I went skating I decided to experiment and try this surrender technique. I brought back the quality of that dream experience into my wakened state. I remembered how I was feeling during the dream and so in the manner of an actor in a role, I "became" the complete skater once again. So I hit the ice . . . and my feet followed my heart. I was free on the ice. That occurred about two and one-half years ago. I've skated with that freedom ever since, and this phenomenon has manifested itself in my roller skating and skiing as well.
>
> —T.R., Arlington, Virginia[6]

REHEARSAL AND DECISION MAKING

Closely related to these mental practice dreams are those that serve a rehearsal function. Most readers will probably have experienced instances of the rehearsal function of dreams. By dreaming about a significant, upcoming event in advance, we can try out various approaches, attitudes, and behaviors, perhaps arriving at a more effective course of action than we otherwise would have. We may also be forewarned of certain potential aspects in a future situation that we otherwise would not have imagined or considered.

In 1975, Dr. William C. Dement confessed that his "wildest speculation" was ". . . that REM sleep and dreaming might have evolved to be utilized in the future" and prophesied that "the eventual function of dreaming will be to allow man to experience the many alternatives of the future in the quasi-reality of the dream, and so make a more 'informed' choice." One of Dement's own dreams provides a striking illustration of how effective this can be:

> Some years ago I was a heavy cigarette smoker—up to two packs a day. Then one night I had an exceptionally vivid and realistic dream in which I had inoperable cancer of the lung. I remember as though it were yesterday looking at the

ominous shadow in my chest X-ray and realizing that the entire right lung was infiltrated. The subsequent physical examination in which a colleague detected widespread metastases . . . was equally vivid. Finally, I experienced the incredible anguish of knowing my life was soon to end, that I would never see my children grow up, and that none of this would have happened if I had quit cigarettes when I first learned of their carcinogenic potential. I will never forget the surprise, joy, and exquisite relief of waking up. I felt I was reborn. Needless to say, the experience was sufficient to induce an immediate cessation of my cigarette habit.[7]

I am happy to report that Dr. Dement is nicotine-free and healthy more than twenty-five years later.

It is clear today that the ecological and political situation of this planet will force upon humanity enormous changes within this coming century. Among the future alternatives are such extremes as have been phrased, "utopia or oblivion." Certainly the planetary situation is one of unprecedented complexity. And just as certainly, what is needed is unprecedented vision: both to avoid catastrophe and to find the path to a better future. And it is the dream that holds the key to this vision, allowing us, in Dement's words, "to experience a future alternative as if it were real, and thereby to provide a supremely enlightened motivation to act upon this knowledge."

Do not forget that we have the freedom to reframe our situation (e.g., mud vs. stars). You have probably heard that the Chinese word for "crisis" is a combination of "danger" and "opportunity." I believe that we would do well to look at these crucial times optimistically, as the age in which humans finally begin to accept responsibility for their actions as well as their dreams.

That puts us now in an era which in terms of the Judeo-Christian creation myth might be regarded as The Eighth Day of the Week. According to the tale unrolled in Genesis, after seven days of hard creative work, God rested. As far as the Bible tells us, He may still be napping. Maybe even—as Hindu theology would have it—Vishnu the Creator is dreaming. So it looks as if it is our turn at the wheel.

WISH FULFILLMENT
"Pleasant dreams!"

Thus we bid each other goodnight. However, according to various surveys, the average dream is *unpleasant.* That average, of course, is of *nonlucid* dreams. As for lucid dreams, the opposite appears to be the case, with the typical emotional valence being unmistakably positive. Many lucid dreamers have remarked on the emotionally rewarding nature of the experience. The lucid dreamer is free to act out impulses that might be impossible in the waking state. Patricia Garfield, in *Pathway to Ecstasy*, has gone so far as to propose that lucid dreams are intrinsically orgasmic. She further speculates that during lucid dreaming the reward or "ecstatic" centers of the brain are being stimulated. This rather fantastic notion may actually find support given evidence linking the neural circuits of REM or paradoxical sleep with the brain's "reward" system.[8] It may be that in certain circumstances lucid dreaming intensifies activity in this intrinsically rewarding system. Whatever the neurophysiological case, lucid dreams are pleasurable experiences.

Lucid dreaming could provide the handicapped and otherwise disadvantaged with the nearest thing to fulfilling their impossible dreams. Paralytics could walk again in their lucid dreams, to say nothing of dancing and flying, and even emotionally fulfilling erotic fantasies. Thus sings the contralto in Handel's *Messiah:*

> *Then shall the eyes of the blind be opened,*
> *and the ears of the deaf unstopped.*
> *Then shall the lame man leap as an hart,*
> *and the tongue of the dumb shall sing!*

LETTING GO: FINISHING UNFINISHED BUSINESS

Resolving difficulties in lucid dreams can help you achieve greater emotional balance and ability to cope with life's troubles. It may help you solve problems of which you were not conscious but that, nonetheless, were limiting your happiness. But lucid dreaming can also be used purposely to address specific difficulties that people are very much aware of. Personal relationships can be the source of some of the most trying problems people face. In many cases, we cannot work through the difficulty with the person involved, and have to deal with it on our own.

When an important relationship ends, people often find that they are left with unresolved issues that cause anxiety and possibly even strain later relationships. In waking life, it is impossible to say those things you never said to your father before he died. And, in waking life, it is often impractical to track down a former mate and work through unresolved issues.

In lucid dreams, however, it is possible to achieve resolution, even if no such possibility exists in the physical world. The absent partner might not be physically present, but he/she can seem phenomenally present. This is enough, since it is your own inner conflicts that you need to settle. Dreams do not raise the dead. But lucid-dream encounters with the dead can appear real enough to allow us to feel we are with them once more, and that they live on in our hearts, as in the following account:

> *My father died of cancer this summer, and I had a long series of dreams in which I was aware that I was dreaming, and insisted that I didn't want to wake up because I was talking to my father, telling him once more that I love him, but he'd insist that I wake up and accept that he was fine and had to go off on his long journey. In a dream I finally saw him off at the station and was relieved that he'd made the train: he'd delayed so long in saying goodbye that he'd almost missed his connections to go off on his wonderful vacation. That was the last dream in the series.*
>
> —Letter to author from C.M. of Framingham, Massachusetts

As Rumi's epitaph reminds us: "When we are dead, seek not our tomb in the earth, but find it in the hearts of men."

5

Lucid Dream Work
From Nightmares to Wholeness

. . .

I could be bounded in a nutshell and
count myself a king of infinite space,
were it not that I have bad dreams.
—SHAKESPEARE

There are no bad dreams.
—BUDDHA

. . .

WHAT ARE NIGHTMARES?

Webster's Revised Unabridged Dictionary defines nightmares as "frightful or oppressive dreams, from which one wakes after extreme anxiety, in a troubled state of mind." To say that nightmares are "bad dreams" seems an understatement, little more controversial than asserting, say, that the devil is evil. After all, nightmares can be among the most terrifying of experiences. Whatever horrors you personally believe to be the worst things that could happen—these are precisely the most likely subjects of your nightmares.

All people, in every age and culture, have suffered from these terrors of the night. People's understanding of the origins of nightmares have varied as much as their understanding of dreams. To some cultures, nightmares were the true experiences of the soul as it wandered another world while the body slept. To others, they were the result of the visitation of demons. Nocturnal experiences, which all but the most skeptical in medieval times would have considered the perverse visitations of demons, might now be interpreted as the equally perverse abductions and "medical" examinations by aliens.

In Western culture today, most people are content to say of nightmares that they are "only dreams," meaning they are imaginary, meaningless, and worthless. That again understates how most of us feel about nightmares; certainly most of us would happily do without the experience.

Not to put too fine a point on it, I believe that this traditional view of nightmares is simply wrong. Yes, nightmares are frightening. But that does not mean they are bad or meaningless, or without positive value. On the contrary, nightmares contain a great deal of potential energy that can provide the impulse for psychological development. Reframing nightmares as opportunities for growth is an important key to learning from your dreams. With a flexible and lucid approach to life, there are no bad dreams.

One of Gary Larson's *The Far Side* cartoons delightfully illustrates this creative approach to experience. Two old ladies behind their locked front door are peering out the window at a "monster from the Id" standing on their doorstep. The wiser of the two ladies says, "Calm down, Edna . . . Yes, it's some giant hideous insect . . . but it could be some giant hideous insect in need of help."[1]

SELF-INTEGRATION, WHOLENESS, AND HEALTH: TAKING RESPONSIBILITY FOR YOUR "DREAMLIFE"

In dreams begin responsibilities.

—W.B. Yeats

Homo sum; humani nil a me alienum puto.
(I am a man; so nothing human is alien to me.)

—Terence, *Heautontimoroumenos*

Since health means increased wholeness, psychological growth often requires the reintegration of neglected or rejected aspects of the personality, and this can be consciously and deliberately achieved through the symbolic encounters of lucid dreaming. The content of a healing dream often takes the form of an integration or union of images. The self-image (or ego) is often unified with elements of what Carl Jung called the "Shadow."

For simplicity, let us divide our personalities into two parts. On one side, we put all of the characteristics we find agreeable and "good." The aggregate of this part of our self forms the self-representation or ego. On the other side, we put all those traits and qualities we consider "bad" or dislike in ourselves and consciously or unconsciously wish to deny. We disown them by projecting them on the mental image of an "other"—the Shadow. Note that the Shadowless self-representation is by design (whether consciously or not) incomplete. According to Jung, when the ego reintegrates, or accepts aspects of the Shadow as parts of itself, it moves toward wholeness and healthy psychological functioning.

Ernest Rossi has proposed that integration, whereby the synthesis of separate psychological structures forms a more comprehensive personality, is a major function of dreaming.[2] Human beings are complex multileveled biopsychosocial systems. Our psyches (the "psycho" level of our system) have many different aspects or subsystems; these different components may or may not be in harmony. Achieving wholeness requires reconciling, or *integrating* all aspects of one's personality. According to Rossi, integration is the primary means by which personality growth takes place:

> *In dreams we witness something more than mere wishes; we experience dramas reflecting our psychological state and the process of change taking place in it. Dreams are a laboratory for experimenting with changes in our psychic life . . . This constructive or synthetic approach to dreams can be clearly stated: Dreaming is an endogenous process of psychological growth, change, and transformation.*[3]

Lucidity can greatly facilitate this process. Lucid dreamers can deliberately identify with and accept, and thereby symbolically integrate, parts of their personalities they had previously rejected or disowned. The stones once rejected by the builder of the ego can then form the new foundation of wholeness. In the same vein, the poet Rainer Maria Rilke surmised, "Perhaps everything that frightens us is, in its deepest essence, something helpless that wants our love."[4] In Jung's view the presence of shadow figures in dreams indicates that the ego model of the self is incomplete. When the ego intentionally accepts the Shadow, it moves toward wholeness and healthy psychological functioning.

The result of failing to accept the shadow aspects of one's personality is illustrated by some of the horrors that plagued Frederik van Eeden's dream life. In the same survey of his dreams in which he coined the term "lucid dream," van Eeden wrote, "In a perfect instance of the lucid dream I float through immensely wide landscapes, with a clear blue, sunny sky, and a feeling of deep bliss and gratitude, which I feel impelled to express by eloquent words of thankfulness and piety."[5] Unfortunately, van Eeden tells us, these beautiful and pious lucid dreams were frequently followed by "demon-dreams," in which he was mocked, harassed, and threatened by what he believed were "intelligent beings of a very low moral order."[6]

Where did these demonic dreams come from? Jung would have probably considered van Eeden's demon-dreams as an example of compensation, striving to correct the mental imbalance produced by his ego's sense of self-righteousness and inflated piety. Friedrich Nietzsche would probably have responded more aphoristically: "If a tree grows up to heaven, its roots reach down to hell." Freud's view was equally clear: "Obviously one must hold oneself responsible for the evil impulses of one's dreams. In what other way can one deal with them? Unless the content of the dream rightly understood is inspired by alien spirits, it is part of my own being."

But for van Eeden to accept the source of these demon-dreams as "part of my own being" was unthinkable. Apparently even more unthinkable than the alternative was an idea van Eeden admitted to be a source of considerable embarrassment: that these demonic holdovers from the Middle Ages actually existed! Was it not after all the twentieth century? Nevertheless, as a dedicated explorer of inner space, he felt compelled to account for their presence in his dreams: it was awkward, but demons they were without question, and logic demanded that if they did not come from inside his mind, they must come from somewhere else. Because he could not bring himself to believe that it was his mind that was responsible for "all the horrors and errors of dreamlife," it must be *someone else*. Thus van Eeden was forced to embrace the demon hypothesis, another variation on "the Devil made me do it." This unfortunate self-defeating belief blocked all efforts to free himself from his demon-dreams.

In his inability to accept responsibility for his dreams, van Eeden was not without illustrious company. Though famously willing to confess all manner of sinful behaviors in every other area of life, Saint Augustine considered dream transgressions to cross a critical line:

> Yet the difference between waking and sleeping is so great that even when, dur-
> ing sleep, [I sin], I return to a clear conscience when I wake and realize that,
> because of this difference, **I was not responsible** for the act, although I am
> sorry that by some means or other it happened to me. [emphasis mine][7]

As near as I can tell, Augustine's position was something like this: I was not responsible for that sinful dream because *it was not* me who did it. If not me, then *who*? (The Shadow.) In the same section of the *Confessions* just quoted, Augustine observes that although he has thoroughly repented his previous life as a sensualist pagan, memories of his sinful habits that have little impact on him while awake powerfully influence his actions while dreaming. With the detached perspective conferred by sixteen centuries, it is easy for us to recognize the Shadow in typical association with a rigid system of morality where all is wrong or right, black or white.

So how does one go about accepting Shadow figures in dreams? There are many approaches, all of which involve entering into a more harmonious relationship with the darker aspects of oneself. One direct and effective approach is to engage Shadow figures in friendly dialogues.[8] This will make a difference with most people you encounter in dreams (or waking life) and might have surprising effects when you try it on threatening figures. Do not slay your dream dragons;

make friends with them. Remember that evil, like beauty, may be in the eye of the beholder. As the Afghan Sufi master, Hakim Sanai, observed 800 years ago:

> If you want the mirror to reflect the face,
> hold it straight and keep it polished bright;
> although the sun does not begrudge its light,
> when seen in a mist it only looks like glass;
> and creatures comelier than angels even
> seem in a dagger to have devil's faces.[9]

To the extent that your thinking is distorted by fear, greed, anger, pride, prejudice, and faulty assumptions, you cannot tell what is really reflected in your consciousness. If your mind resembles a fun house mirror, do not be surprised if in your dream an angel seems a demon. Therefore, you would do well to assume the best. When you meet a monster in your lucid dream, sincerely greet him like a long lost friend, and that is what he will be.

The nearest thing I have had to a demon-dream was the "riot in the classroom" lucid dream introduced in Chapter 1, in which I successfully accepted and integrated one of my demons—the repulsive ogre. It seems clear on several levels that this was a healing dream. In the first place, the initial conflict, an unhealthy condition of stress, was resolved positively. Also, the dream ego was able to accept the ogre as a part of itself, and thus move toward wholeness. Finally, there is more direct evidence—the feeling of increased wholeness and well-being that I experienced upon awakening.

I believe that the feelings you wake up with after a lucid dream reliably indicate your intuitive evaluation of how you did in that dream. If you have done something in a lucid dream that you feel good about on waking, you should repeat that action in future lucid dreams. If you feel bad about some action, then avoid doing it in subsequent lucid dreams. Following this policy, of course, will lead to increasingly good feelings in your lucid dreams—and also upon awakening.

FACING THE NIGHTMARE

> *Do the thing you fear most and the death of fear is certain.*
>
> —Mark Twain

> *There is no cause for fear. It is imagination, blocking you as a wooden bolt holds the door. Burn that bar . . .*
>
> —Rumi

Fear of the unknown is worse than fear of the known, and this seems nowhere more true than in dreams. Thus, one of the most adaptive responses to an unpleasant dream situation is to face it, as can be seen in the following account of a series of nightmares experienced by the nineteenth-century lucid dream pioneer, the Marquis d'Hervey de Saint-Denys:

> *I was not aware that I was dreaming, and imagined I was being pursued by abominable monsters. I was fleeing through an endless series of rooms. I had difficulty in opening the doors that divided them, and no sooner had I closed each door behind me than I heard it opened again by the hideous procession of monsters. They were uttering horrible cries as they tried to catch me; I felt they were gaining on me. I awoke with a start, panting and bathed in sweat.*[10]

This same nightmare, "with all its attendant terrors," recurred four times in the course of six weeks. But "on the fourth occurrence of the nightmare," the Marquis wrote,

> *Just as the monsters were about to start pursuing me again, I suddenly became aware of my true situation. My desire to rid myself of these illusory terrors gave me the strength to overcome my fear. I did not flee, but instead, making a great effort of will, I put my back up against the wall, and determined to look the phantom monsters full in the face. This time I would make a deliberate study of them, and not just glance at them, as I had on previous occasions.*[11]

In spite of his lucidity, the Marquis "experienced a fairly violent emotional shock at first," explaining, "The appearance in dreams of something one has been dreading to see can still have a considerable effect on one's mind, even when one is forewarned against it."[12] Nevertheless, the intrepid lucid dreamer continued:

> I stared at my principal assailant. He bore some resemblance to one of those bristling and grimacing demons which are sculptured on cathedral porches. Academic curiosity soon overcame all my other emotions. I saw the fantastic monster halt a few paces from me, hissing and leaping about. Once I had mastered my fear his actions appeared merely burlesque. I noticed the claws on one of his hands, or paws, I should say. There were seven in all, each very precisely delineated. The monster's features were all precise and realistic: hair and eyebrows, what looked like a wound on his shoulder, and many other details. In fact, I would class this as one of the clearest images I had had in dreams. Perhaps this image was based on a memory of some Gothic bas-relief.
> . . . The result of concentrating my attention on this figure was that all his acolytes vanished, as if by magic. Soon the leading monster also began to slow down, lose precision, and take on a downy appearance. He finally changed into a sort of floating hide, which resembled the faded costumes used as street signs by fancy dress shops at carnival time. Some unremarkable scenes followed, and finally I woke up.[13]

After such a complete undoing, the deconstructed monster—proven nothing more than an empty suit woven from fancy and fear—never again left the archetypical costume shop to disturb the Marquis's slumbers.

Paul Tholey has also reported that when the dream ego looks courageously and openly at hostile dream figures, their appearance often becomes less threatening. If, on the contrary, one attempts to make a dream figure disappear, it may become *more* threatening, as in the following case reported by G. Scott Sparrow in his seminal *Lucid Dreaming: Dawning of the Clear Light*:

I am standing in the hallway outside my room. It is night and hence dark where I stand. Dad comes in the front door. I tell him that I am there so as not to frighten him or provoke an attack. I am afraid for no apparent reason. I look outside through the door and see a dark figure, which appears to be a large animal. I point at it in fear. The animal, which is a huge, black panther, comes through the doorway. I reach out to it with both hands, extremely afraid. Placing my hands on its head, I say, "You're only a dream." But I am half pleading in my statement and cannot dispel my fear. I pray for Jesus' presence and protection. But the fear is still with me as I awaken.[14]

Here the dreamer uses his marginal lucidity to try to make his frightful image disappear. I say "marginal" precisely because with full lucidity, the dreamer understands that it is irrational to try to escape the "dangers" of the dream. Acting as if dream images are actually dangerous undermines our lucidity. Would you be thinking clearly if you feared that a picture of a snake could actually bite you? And if a picture, or a movie, or a dream image could hurt you, why stop there? What would you think of yourself if you threw down this book when you saw the image to the right? Or if you read, "Asklepios, the Greek god of healing was believed to take the form of a *snake*"?[15]

Enough, or too much! The word "snake" has no fangs. The dream is not the thing any more or less than the word is.

Likewise, as a dream, the huge, black panther was less dangerous than a kitten. But the fearful, half-pleading statement, "You're only a dream," implied, "I really *hope* you're *only* a dream!" Fear is your worst enemy in dreams; if you allow it to persist, it will grow stronger and your self confidence *as well as your lucidity* will grow correspondingly weaker.

Novice lucid dreamers may initially use their new powers to find more clever ways to escape their fears. This is because of our natural tendency to continue in our current frame of mind. If in a dream in which you are fleeing from harm you realize you are dreaming, you will still tend to continue escaping, even though you should now know that there is nothing to flee from. During the first six months of my personal record of lucid dreaming, I occasionally suffered from this sort of mental inertia until the following dream inspired a permanent change in my lucid dreaming behavior:

> Escaping from some forgotten danger, I was climbing down the side of a skyscraper, gripping the walls like a lizard. It occurred to me that I could better escape by flying away, and as I did so, I realized that I was dreaming. By the time I reached the ground, the dream and my lucidity faded. Instead of waking up in bed, I found myself sitting in the audience of a lecture hall, privileged to be hearing Idries Shah, an eminent Sufi teacher, comment on my dream. "It was good that Stephen realized he was dreaming and could fly," Shah observed with a bemused tone, "but too bad that he didn't see that, because it was a dream, there was no need to escape and nothing to flee."

This account should make it very clear that while I do not believe that dreams in general are messages, equally I do not believe that dreams never contain messages! Suffice it to say, I got the message. After this dream lecture, I resolved never to use my lucidity to avoid unpleasant situations. But I was not going to be content to passively avoid conflicts by doing nothing. I made a firm resolution regarding my lucid dreaming behavior. Anytime I became lucid I would ask myself two questions: First, have I been avoiding or running away from anything in the dream? And second, was there any conflict in the dream? If the answer to either question was yes, then I would face whatever I had been avoiding and resolve any conflict. I have remembered this principle in almost every subsequent lucid dream and have attempted to resolve conflicts and face my fears whenever it was called for.

Escaping from a nightmare by awakening only suppresses your conscious awareness of the anxiety-provoking imagery. You may feel a certain relief, but like the prisoner who digs through his prison wall and finds himself in the cell next door, you have not really escaped. Moreover, aware of it or not, you are left with an unresolved conflict that will doubtless come back to haunt you some other night. In addition, you may have an unpleasant and unhealthy emotional state with which to start your day.

If, on the other hand, you choose to stay in the nightmare rather than waking from it, you can resolve the conflict in a way that brings you increased self-confidence and improved mental health. Then, when you wake up, you will feel that you have freed some extra energy with which to begin your day with new confidence.

Tholey, who has researched the effectiveness of various attitudes toward hostile dream characters, concludes that a conciliatory approach is most likely to result in a positive outcome. His conciliatory method is based on the practice of engaging in dialogues with dream characters (see exercise "Dialoguing with Dream Characters" on the following page). He found that when dreamers tried to reconcile with hostile figures, the figures often transformed from "lower order into higher order creatures," meaning from beasts or mythological beings into humans, and that these transformations "often allowed the subjects to immediately understand the meaning of the dream." Furthermore, conciliatory behavior toward threatening figures would generally cause them to look and act in a friendlier manner. For example, Tholey himself dreamed:

I became lucid, while being chased by a tiger, and wanted to flee. I then pulled myself back together, stood my ground, and asked, "Who are you?" The tiger was taken aback but transformed into my father and answered, "I am your father and will now tell you what you are to do!" In contrast to my earlier dreams, I did not attempt to beat him but tried to get involved in a dialogue with him. I told him that he could not order me around. I rejected his threats and insults. On the other hand, I had to admit that some of my father's criticism was justified, and I decided to change my behavior accordingly. At that moment my father became friendly, and we shook hands. I asked him if he could help me, and he encouraged me to go my own way alone. My father then seemed to slip into my own body, and I remained alone in the dream.[16]

To encourage a good dialogue, it is best to treat dream figures as equals. Questions like the following, posed in a non-threatening tone, may open up fruitful lines of dialogue: Who are you? Who am I? Why are you here? Why are you acting the way you are? What do you have to tell me? What do I most need to know? Can you help me? Can I help you?

EXERCISE: DIALOGUING WITH DREAM CHARACTERS

1 **Practice imaginary dialogues in the waking state.** Choose a recent dream in which you had an unpleasant encounter with a dream figure. Get a piece of paper and pen to write down the conversation you imagine. Envision yourself talking to the dream character; visualize the character before you. Begin a dialogue by asking questions. You may choose a question from the list above or substitute any personally relevant question. Write down your questions and the responses you get from the character. Try not to let critical thoughts interrupt the flow, such as "This is silly," or "I'm just making this up," or "That's not true." Listen and interact. You can evaluate later. Terminate the dialogue when it runs out of energy or when you achieve a useful resolution. Then evaluate the conversation and ask yourself what you did right and what you would do differently next time. Once you are successful with this, try the same exercise on another dream.

2 **Set your intention.** Set a goal for yourself that the next time you have a disturbing encounter with a dream character you will become lucid and engage the character in dialogue.

3 **Dialogue with problem dream figures.** When you encounter anyone with whom you feel conflict, ask yourself whether or not you are dreaming. If you find that you are dreaming, continue as follows: Stay and face the character, and begin a dialogue with one of the opening questions from the list above. Listen to the character's responses, and try to address his, her, or its problems as well as your own. See if you can come to an agreement or make friends.

Continue the dialogue until you reach a comfortable resolution. Then, be sure to awaken while you still remember the conversation clearly, and write it down.

4 **Evaluate the dialogue.** Ask yourself if you achieved the best result you could. Think about how you could improve your results. You could use Step 1 to relive the dialogue to attain a more satisfying result.

In contrast to the positive results of conciliatory dialogue, Tholey found that when dreamers attacked dream characters either verbally or physically, the dream figures often regressed in form, for instance from a mother to a witch, then to a beast. We might assume that the other characters in our dream worlds are more helpful as friendly humans than as subdued animals, so the aggressive approach may not be the best choice most of the time.

I say most of the time because in some instances it may not be advisable to open yourself to a dream attacker. In the case of dreams that replay real life events in which one was abused by someone—a rapist or child molester, for example—a more satisfying resolution may result from overcoming, disarming, and transforming the dream attacker. However, in many instances, Tholey's research has shown that aggressive attacks on dream characters can result in feelings of anxiety or guilt, and the subsequent emergence of dream "avengers." So I would advise avoiding such behavior unless it truly seems the best option.

I have a few suggestions to add to these ideas about how to resolve nightmare situations. One is an extension of the "confront and conquer" approach. Though I cannot wholly recommend conquering dream characters, the intention to confront all danger in dreams is fully in accordance with my concept of a constructive dreamlife. Remember that nothing can hurt you in dreams, and consider whether there is any reason why you should not allow yourself to experience the things you are trying to avoid in the dream.

In an excellent example, a woman dreamed she had difficulty avoiding being struck by cars as she crossed a busy street. As she had an unusually intense fear of traffic in waking life, upon becoming lucid she decided to directly confront her fear and leaped into the path of an oncoming pickup truck. She described that she felt the truck pass through her and then she, in an ethereal form, rose heavenward, feeling elevated and amused.

This passive, nonviolent, "let it happen" approach may not be best when dealing with dream characters, however. In Tholey's research, "Defenseless behavior almost always led to unpleasant experiences of fear or discouragement."[17] Hostile dream figures would tend to grow in size and strength relative to the dreamer. The reason for this may be that dream characters often are projections of ourselves, and by giving in to their attacks, we may be allowing untransformed negative energies within us to overpower our better aspects.

You do not need to talk to shadow figures to make peace with them. If you can find it in your heart to genuinely love your dream enemies, they become your friends. Embracing the rejected with loving acceptance symbolically integrates the shadow into the self-model, as illustrated by my "embracing the ogre" dream quoted in Chapter 1.

RECURRENT NIGHTMARES

When thinking about a nightmare becomes so painful that we avoid it, it is not surprising that it recurs. In contrast, even the most terrible images become less frightening when we examine them. More than a century ago, and definitely ahead of his time, Hervey de Saint-Denys clearly described the mechanism of recurrent nightmares in the following comment on his living gargoyle dream, quoted earlier in this chapter:

> I don't know the origin of the dream. Probably some pathological cause brought it on the first time; but afterwards, when it was repeated on several occasions in the space of six weeks, it was clearly brought back solely by the impressions it had made on me and by my instinctive fear of seeing it again. If I happened, when dreaming, to find myself in a closed room, the memory of this horrible dream was immediately revived; I would glance toward the door, the thought

of what I was afraid of seeing was enough to produce the sudden appearance of the same terrors, in the same form as before.[18]

In agreement with Saint-Denys, I believe nightmares become recurrent by the following process: In the first place, the dreamer awakens from a nightmare in a state of intense anxiety and fear; naturally, he or she hopes that it will never happen again. The wish to avoid at all costs the events of the nightmare ensures that they will be remembered. Later, something in the person's waking life associated with the original dream causes the person to dream about a situation similar to the original nightmare. The dreamer recognizes, perhaps unconsciously, the similarity, and thus expects the same thing to happen. Thus, expectation causes the dream to follow the first plot, and the more the dream recurs, the more likely it is to recur in the same form. Looking at recurrent nightmares in this way suggests a simple treatment: the dreamer can imagine a new conclusion for the dream to weaken the expectation that it has only one possible outcome.

Several years ago, I used a similar approach with someone suffering from recurrent nightmares. A man telephoned the Stanford Sleep Disorders Clinic asking for help. He feared going to sleep because he might have "that terrible dream" again. In his dream, he told me, he would find himself in a room in which the walls were closing in, threatening to crush him. He would desperately try to open the door, which would always be locked.

I asked him to imagine he was back in the dream, knowing it was a dream. What else could he do? At first he was unable to think of anything else that could possibly happen, so I modeled what I was asking him to do. I imagined I was in the same dream, and I visualized the walls closing in. However, the moment I found the door locked, it occurred to me to reach into my pocket, where I found the key, with which I unlocked the door and walked out. I recounted my imagined solution and asked him to try again. He imagined the dream again—this time he looked around the room and noticed that there was no ceiling and climbed out.

I suggested to him that if this dream should ever recur, he could recognize it as a dream and remember his solution. I asked him to call me if the dream came back, but he never did. Unfortunately, we cannot be sure about what happened. But I think that having found some way to cope with that particular (dream) situation, he had no need to dream about it again because he no longer feared it. As I have discussed previously in this book and elsewhere, we dream about what we expect to happen, both what we fear and what we hope for.

Rehearsal redreaming is done while awake. However, a similar technique can be practiced during the recurrent nightmare, if the dreamer is lucid. Instead of imagining how the dream might turn out if the dreamer tried something new, while lucid, the dreamer can try the alternative action right there in the nightmare. The resultant resolution should be all the more empowering, because of the enhanced reality of the dream experience. Practicing altering the course of recurrent nightmares both in waking and dreaming may be even more effective. Sometimes, the waking redreaming exercise is enough to resolve the problem created in the dream so that it never recurs again. However, if the dream does occur again, then the dreamer should be prepared to become lucid and consciously face the problem. The exercise below incorporates both reentry techniques.

EXERCISE: REDREAMING RECURRENT NIGHTMARES [19]

1 **Recall and record the recurrent nightmare.** If you have had a particular nightmare more than once, recall it in as much detail as you can and write it down. Examine it for points where you could influence the turn of events by doing something differently.
2 **Choose a reentry point and new action.** Choose a specific part of the dream to change, and a specific new action that you would like to try at that point to alter the course of the dream. Also select the most relevant point before the trouble spot at which to reenter the dream.
3 **Relax completely.** Find a time and place where you can be alone and uninterrupted for ten to twenty minutes. In a comfortable position, close your eyes and relax completely.

4 **Redream the nightmare, seeking resolution.** Beginning at the entry point you chose in Step 2, imagine you are back in the dream. Visualize the dream happening as it did until you reach the part at which you have chosen to try a new behavior. See yourself doing the new action, and then continue imagining the dream until you discover what effect your alteration has on its outcome.

5 **Evaluate your redreamed resolution.** When the imagined dream has ended, open your eyes. Write down what happened as if it were a normal dream report. Note how you feel about the new dream resolution. If you are not satisfied and still feel uncomfortable about the dream, try the exercise again with a new alternative action. Possibly, achieving a comfortable resolution with the waking exercise will be enough to stop the recurrence of the nightmare.

6 **If the dream recurs, follow your redreamed plan of action.** If the dream occurs again, do in the dream what you visualized during waking reentry. Remember that the dream cannot harm you, and be firmly resolved to carry through with your new behavior.

CHILDREN'S NIGHTMARES

Children tend to have more nightmares than adults, but fortunately they appear to have little difficulty putting into practice the idea of facing their fears with lucid dreaming, as I can attest from my own experience. Once, when I was making long-distance small talk with my niece, I asked her about her dreams. Madeleina, then seven years old, burst out with the description of a fearful nightmare. She had dreamed that she had gone swimming, as she often did, in the local reservoir. But this time, she had been threatened and terrified by a shark. I sympathized with her fear and added, matter-of-factly, "But of course you know there aren't really any sharks in Colorado." She replied, "Of course not!" So, I continued, "Well, since you know there aren't really any sharks where you swim, if you ever see one there again, it would be because you were dreaming. And, of course, a dream shark can't really do you any harm. It is only frightening if you don't know that it's a dream. But once you know you're dreaming, you can do whatever you like—you could even make friends with the dream shark, if you wanted to! Why not give it a try?" Madeleina seemed intrigued. A week later, she telephoned to proudly announce, "Do you know what I did? I rode on the back of the shark!"

Whether or not this approach to children's nightmares always produces such impressive results we do not yet know, but it is certainly worth exploring. If you are a parent with children suffering from nightmares, you should first make sure that they know what a dream is and then tell them about lucid dreaming. For more information on children's nightmares and how to treat them, see Patricia Garfield's excellent book *Your Child's Dreams*.

That lucid dreaming promises to banish one of the terrors of childhood seems reason enough for all enlightened parents to teach the method to their children. In addition, an important bonus of the lucid dreaming approach to children's nightmares is that it results in an increased sense of mastery and self-confidence, as can be seen in all of the examples above. Think of the value of discovering that fear has no more power than you let it have, and that you are the master.

6

Life as a Dream

Awake in Your Dreams
and Alive in Your Life

. . .

We shall not cease from exploration
And the end of all our exploring
Will be to arrive where we started
And know the place for the first time.
Through the unknown, remembered gate
When the last of earth left to discover
Is that which was the beginning.
—T. S. ELIOT, "LITTLE GIDDING," *FOUR QUARTETS*

. . .

A VEHICLE FOR EXPLORING REALITY

Dreams are a reservoir of knowledge and experience, yet they are often over-looked as a vehicle for exploring reality.

—Tarthang Tulku, *Openness Mind*

For more than a thousand years, the Tibetan Buddhists have used lucid dreaming as a means of experiencing the illusory nature of personal reality and as one part of a set of practices said to lead to enlightenment and the discovery of the ultimate nature of the self.

The Sufis may also use lucid dreaming, or something like it, for spiritual purposes. The famous twelfth-century Spanish Sufi Muhiyuddin Ibn El-Arabi reportedly recommended, "A person must control his thoughts in a dream. The training of this alertness . . . will produce great benefits for the individual. Everyone should apply himself to the attainment of this ability of such great value."[1]

Tarthang Tulku explains the benefits of lucid dreaming as follows:

Experiences we gain from practices we do during our dream time can then be brought into our daytime experience. For example, we can learn to change the frightening images we see in our dreams into peaceful forms. Using the same process, we can transmute the negative emotions we feel during the daytime into increased awareness. Thus we can use our dream experiences to develop a more flexible life.[2]

"With continuing practice," Tarthang Tulku explains,

. . . we see less and less difference between the waking and the dream state. Our experiences in waking life become more vivid and varied, the result of a lighter and more refined awareness . . . This kind of awareness, based on dream practice, can help create an inner balance.[3]

For Tibetan dream yogis, the lucid dream, as "a vehicle for exploring reality," represents an opportunity to experiment with and realize the subjective nature of the dream state and by extension waking experience as well. They regard such a realization as bearing the profoundest possible significance.

Realizing that our experience of reality is subjective, rather than direct and true, may have practical implications. According to Tarthang Tulku, when we think of all of our experiences as being subjective, and therefore like a dream, "the concepts and self-identities which have boxed us in begin to fall away. As our self-identity becomes less rigid, our problems become lighter. At the same time, a much deeper level of awareness develops." As a result, "even the hardest things become enjoyable and easy. When you realize that everything is like a dream, you attain pure awareness. And the way to attain this awareness is to realize that all experience is like a dream."[4]

As a result of practicing lucid dreaming, continues Tarthang Tulku, "our experiences in waking life become more vivid and varied. This kind of awareness, based on dream practice can help create an inner balance" that not only "nourishes the mind in a way that nurtures the whole living organism," but "illumines previously unseen facets of the mind and lights the way for us to explore ever-new dimensions of reality." Moreover, and directly to the point at hand, lucid dreaming practice can be used to "learn to change ourselves" and "to develop a more flexible attitude."[5]

SELF-KNOWLEDGE

Nasrudin went into a bank to cash a check. The teller asked him if he could identify himself. "Yes, I can . . . " Nasrudin replied, taking out a mirror with which he scrutinizes his features, "that's me all right."
　　　　—Idries Shah, *The Subtleties of the Inimitable Mulla Nasrudin*

Who we really are is not necessarily the same as who we identify ourselves with. We are not who we think we are in our dreams (or indeed while awake). You can readily observe this fact for yourself in your next lucid dream. Ask yourself about the nature of each thing you find in your lucid dream. For example, you may be sitting at a dream table, with your feet on the dream floor; and yes, that is a dream shoe, on a dream foot, part of a dream body, so this must be a dream me! All you need to do is to reflect on your situation in a lucid dream and you see that the person you appear to be in the dream cannot be who you really are: it is only an image, a mental model of your self, or, to use the Freudian term, your ego.

Seeing that the ego cannot be who you really are makes it easy to stop identifying with it. Once you no longer identify with your ego, you are freer to change it. The recognition that the ego is a simplified model of the self gives you a more accurate model of the self and makes it more difficult for you to mistake the map for the territory.

If you can see your ego objectively in its proper role as the representation and servant of the self, you will not need to struggle with your ego. You cannot get rid of it in any case, nor would it be desirable to do so—the ego is necessary for effective functioning in the world. The fact that both ego and self say, "I," is a source of confusion and misidentification. The well-informed ego says truly, "I am what I know myself to be." The self says merely, "I am." If I know that I am not my ego, I am detached enough to be objective about myself, as in the Sufi story in which a monk boasts to Nasrudin, "I am so detached that I never think of myself, only of others." Nasrudin replies, "Well, I am so objective that I can look at myself as if I were another person; so I can afford to think of myself."[6]

The less we identify with who we think we are, the more likely we are to discover who we really are. In this regard, the Sufi master Tariqavi wrote,

> *When you have found yourself you can have knowledge. Until then you can only have opinions. Opinions are based on habit and what you conceive to be convenient.*
>
> *The study of the Way requires self-encounter along the way. You have not met yourself yet. The only advantage of meeting others in the meantime is that one of them may present you to yourself.*
>
> *Before you do that, you will possibly imagine that you have met yourself many times. But the truth is that when you do meet yourself, you come into a permanent endowment and bequest of knowledge that is like no other experience on earth.*[7]

Before feeling the sincere desire to "meet yourself," you may find the fulfillment of your ego's wants and wishes far more compelling. This is natural, and it would probably be counter-productive and frustrating for you to try to pursue more sublime aspects of yourself when part of you is still crying for the satisfaction of drives and passions unsatiated in waking life.

Likewise, you should not seek transcendence as a means of escapism. Remember van Eeden's demon-dreams. You must first be willing to deal with whatever problems you may find on your personal level. But after having resolved any problems within the dream, and after a sufficient amount of wish-fulfillment activity, you may feel the urge or need to seek possibilities beyond what you have known or conceived.

To go beyond the ego's model of the world, the lucid dreamer must relinquish control of the dream—surrender—to something beyond the ego. One of my most memorable and personally meaningful lucid dreams occurred when I opened myself to guidance from "The Highest":

Late one morning several years ago, I found myself driving in my sports car down a dream road, delighted by the vibrantly beautiful scenery, and perfectly aware that I was dreaming. After driving a short distance farther, I saw a very attractive hitchhiker on the side of the road just ahead. I hardly need to say that I felt strongly inclined to stop and pick her up. But I said to myself, "I've had that dream before. How about something new?" So I passed her by, resolving instead to seek "The Highest." As soon as I opened myself to guidance, my car took off into the air, flying rapidly upwards, until it fell behind, like the first stage of a rocket, and I continued to fly higher into the clouds. I passed a cross on a steeple top, a star of David, and other religious symbols. As I rose still higher, beyond the clouds, I entered a space that seemed a limitless mystical realm: a vast emptiness that was overflowing with love, an unbounded space that felt somehow like home. My mood had lifted as high as I had flown, and I began to sing with ecstatic inspiration. The quality of my voice was truly amazing—it spanned the entire range from deepest bass to highest soprano. I felt as if I were embracing the entire cosmos in the resonance of my voice.[8]

This dream gave me a new sense of identity. I felt as if I had discovered another form of being to which my ordinary sense of self stood in relation as a drop of water to the sea. Of course, I have no way of evaluating how close this vision comes to the ultimate nature of reality (if there is any such thing), and I say this in spite of the conviction of certainty that came with the experience.

ARE WE AWAKE?

Idries Shah, considered by some to have been the Sufi Teacher of the Age, said that most people make the fundamental mistake of thinking that we are alive when we have "merely fallen asleep in life's waiting room."[9] Indeed, it is a traditional doctrine of esoteric psychologies that the ordinary state of consciousness we call "waking" is so far from seeing things as they are in "Objective Reality" that it could be more accurately called "sleep" or "dreaming." Bertrand Russell, after traveling a very different path, arrives at much the same conclusion: "If modern physics is to be believed," writes the philosopher, "the dreams we call waking perceptions have only a very little more resemblance to objective reality than the fantastic dreams of sleep."[10]

But philosophers aside, if you were asked, "Are you awake *now*?" you would probably reply, "Certainly!" Unfortunately, feeling certain that we are awake provides no guarantee that we *are* in fact awake. When Samuel Johnson kicked a stone as if to say, "We *know* what's real," he was expressing this sense of certainty. Yet Dr. Johnson could have dreamed he kicked a stone and felt the same. The illusory sense of certainty about the completeness and coherence of our lives leads us to what William James described as a "premature closing of our accounts with reality."[11]

How do you know that you are awake right now? You may say you remember waking up from your last night's sleep. But that might merely have been a "false awakening," and you might have been fooled by dreaming you are not dreaming anymore. Perhaps what we take to be "true awakenings" are really just another degree of partial or false awakenings. A novelist has similarly argued:

Why, my friend, should these successive degrees not exist? I have often dreamt that I was awakening from a dream, and in a dream I have reflected on the preceding dream: on waking, I was then able to reflect on my two dreams. Owing to its greater clearness, the second one was a sort of waking in relation of the first. And as for this real waking, who is to say that it will not appear to me as a dream one day in its turn in relation to an even clearer view of the sequence of things . . . ? So many things here below remain confused and obscure to us; it is impossible that the true waking state lies here.[12]

Once more, try to really ask yourself, "Am I awake?"

You will note how difficult it is to genuinely raise the question. To sincerely ask whether we are really awake requires honest doubt—however slight. And this is no easy matter for most of us. But doubting the indubitable is the business of philosophers. As Nietzsche put it, " . . . the man of philosophic turn has a foreboding that underneath this reality in which we live and have our being, another and altogether different reality lies concealed, and that therefore it is also an appearance."[13] Indeed, Schopenhauer considered his own propensity to at times regard people and things alike "as mere phantoms and dream-pictures" as the very criterion of philosophic ability.[14]

How might we not be fully awake? It may be that we possess a higher sense (let us say, a form of intuition) that ordinarily remains asleep when our lesser, though better known, senses awake. Thus, as was suggested above, the experience we call "awakening" and consider complete may in fact be only a partial awakening. As A. R. Orage has written,

> It may be feared that there is something morbid in the foregoing speculations; and that an effort to see our waking life as merely a special form of sleep must diminish its importance for us and ours for it. But this attitude toward a possible and probable fact is itself morbidly timid. The truth is that just as in night-dreams the first symptom of waking is to suspect that one is dreaming, the first symptom of waking from the waking state—the second awaking of religion—is the suspicion that our present waking state is dreaming likewise. To be aware that we are only partially awake is the first condition of becoming and making ourselves more fully awake.[15]

Given that mere philosophical reasoning has little power to genuinely raise the suspicion that we are only partially awake, it is fortunate that we can come to this understanding through direct experience. Lucid dreams plainly show us what it is like to think we are awake, and then to discover that we are not. Professor J. H. M. Whiteman's book *The Mystical Life* provides an example of the astonishing impact this discovery can bring. Dr. Whiteman believed that his nocturnal mystical experience was stimulated by the meditative state in which he listened to the performance of a celebrated string quartet on the previous evening. The concert so moved him that for a few moments he felt "rapt out of space by the extreme beauty of the music," experiencing "a new state of contemplation and joy." If this sounds like a peak experience, his first dream of the following night revealed another range of mountains towering beyond:

> *I seemed to move smoothly through a region of space where, presently, a vivid sense of cold flowed in on me and held my attention with a strange interest. I believe that at that moment the dream had become lucid. Then suddenly, . . . all that up to now had been wrapped in confusion instantly passed away, and a new space burst forth in vivid presence and utter reality, with perception free and pinpointed as never before; the darkness itself seemed alive. The thought that was then borne in upon me with inescapable conviction was this: "I have never been awake before."* [16]

While it is unusual for lucid dreamers to experience as deep a sense of topsy-turvy transformation of the familiar to the strange as Whiteman's "I have never been awake before," it is not at all unusual for them to feel they have never before been fully awake and present in their dreams.

The experience of lucid dreaming provides a simple but powerful analogy for understanding degrees of awakening. Solve for X: as ordinary dreaming is to lucid dreaming, so the ordinary waking state is to X. This unknown state X, the "lucid waking state," may be interpreted in various ways ranging from simple mindfulness or cognizance to enlightenment. Remember that there are degrees of lucidity, ranging from the marginal to complete, as our knowledge of the meaning of being in a dream varies from knowing only that this is not everyday reality to all the implications of the state, however many there may be. Likewise, there will be similar degrees of understanding with regard to being in the dream we call life.

This capacity to introduce us to the possibility of a fuller awakening may prove to be lucid dreaming's most profound application. Certainly, it provides the greatest value in helping us become more alive in our lives.

We all have had the experience of going into a room to do or get something or other and forgetting when we get there what it was we had intended to do. Worse yet, we may not even notice that we have forgotten why we were there, and instead just do something we habitually do in that room. This trivial bit of the psychopathology of everyday life offers a compelling analogy to the amnesia we experience not just in dreams but in our lives as a whole. Just as in dreams where we typically neither remember what we were doing before the dream began (e.g., going to sleep, etc.), nor concern ourselves with the fact that we cannot recall, so in life. We find ourselves alive, here, now, with no recollection of what we came to do, or even who or *that* we were "before we were." Who? Whence? To what end? We have no clue.

Or do we? Just as we are able with appropriate help and preparation to remember ourselves and our intentions in our dreams, so we can remember what we are here to do in our lives. Let me leave you with a clue. T. S. Eliot unveiled half the secret with the words, "In my beginning is my end," and the other half as well, with the reflection, "In my end is my beginning."[17]

Speaking of beginnings and ends, I am reminded of a tale said to contain in the various levels of its interpretation "all wisdom." Perhaps you have heard it before?

THE PRECIOUS JEWEL

In a remote realm of perfection, there was a just monarch who had a wife and a wonderful son and daughter. They all lived together in happiness.

One day the father called his children before him and said:

"The time has come, as it does for all. You are to go down, an infinite distance, to another land. You shall seek and find and bring back a precious Jewel."

The travelers were conducted in disguise to a strange land, whose inhabitants almost all lived a dark existence. Such was the effect of this place that the two lost touch with each other, wandering as if asleep.

From time to time they saw phantoms, similitudes of their country and of the Jewel, but such was their condition that these things only increased the depth of their reveries, which they now began to take as reality.

When news of his children's plight reached the king, he sent word by a trusted servant, a wise man:

"Remember your mission, awaken from your dream, and remain together."

With this message they roused themselves, and with the help of their rescuing guide they dared the monstrous perils which surrounded the Jewel, and by its magic aid returned to their realm of light, to remain in increased happiness for evermore.[18]

Notes

...

1 In Dreams Awake

1. S. LaBerge, *Lucid Dreaming* (Los Angeles: Jeremy P. Tarcher, Inc., 1985), 1–2.

2. T. Tulku, *Openness Mind* (Berkeley: Dharma Press, 1978), 74.

3. G. S. Sparrow, *Lucid Dreaming: Dawning of the Clear Light* (Virginia Beach: A.R.E. Press, 1978), 26–27.

4. I. Shah, *Seeker After Truth* (London: Octagon Press, 1982), 33.

2 A Psychobiological Model of Dreaming

1. Dalai Lama, *The Joy of Living and Dying in Peace* (HarperSanFrancisco, 1997), 169.

2. S. LaBerge, *Lucid Dreaming* (Los Angeles: Jeremy P. Tarcher, Inc., 1985).

3 Learning Lucid Dreaming

1. For information on lucid dreaming training, visit www.lucidity.com.

2. Dalai Lama, *Sleeping, Dreaming, and Dying: An Exploration of Consciousness with the Dalai Lama XIV,* ed. F. Varela (Boston: Wisdom, 1997), 107.

4 The Practical Dreamer: Applications of Lucid Dreaming

1. E. Green, A. Green, and D. Walters, "Biofeedback for Mind-Body Self-Regulation: Healing and Creativity," *Fields within Fields . . . within Fields* (New York: Stulman, 1972), 144.

2. S. LaBerge and H. Rheingold, *Exploring the World of Lucid Dreaming* (New York: Ballantine 1990), 223.

3. D. T. Jaffe and D. E. Bresler, "The Use of Guided Imagery As an Adjunct to Medical Diagnosis and Treatment," *Journal of Humanistic Psychology* 20 (1980): 45–59.

4. B. M. Kedrov, "On the Question of Scientific Creativity," *Voprosy Psikologii* 3 (1957): 91–113.

5. W. Dement, *Some Must Watch While Some Must Sleep* (San Francisco: W. H. Freeman, 1972), 101.

6. S. LaBerge, *Lucid Dreaming* (Los Angeles: Tarcher, 1985), 1–2.

7. W. Dement, Op. cit., 102.

8. S. S. Steiner and S. J. Ellman, "Relation between REM Sleep and Intracranial Self-Stimulation," *Science* 177 (1972): 1122–24.

5 Lucid Dream Work: From Nightmares to Wholeness

1. G. Larson, *Beyond the Far Side* (Kansas City: Andrews, McMeel & Parker 1983).

2. E. Rossi, *Dreams and the Growth of Personality* (New York: Bruner/Mazel 1972/1985).

3. Ibid., 142.

4. R. Rilke, *Letters to a Young Poet* (New York: Random House 1984), 91–92.

5. F. van Eeden, "A Study of Dreams," *Proceedings of the Society for Psychical Research* 26 (1913): 439.

6. Ibid., 461.

7. Augustine, *Confessions*, X, 30.

8. P. Tholey, "A Model of Lucidity Training As a Means of Self-Healing and Psychological Growth," *Conscious Mind, Sleeping Brain,* eds. J. Gackenbach and S. LaBerge (New York: Plenum 1988), 263–287.

9. H. Sanai, *The Walled Garden of Truth,* trans. D. Pendlebury, (New York: Dutton 1976), 11.

10. H. Saint-Denys, *Dreams and How to Guide Them* (London: Duckworth 1982), 58–59.

11. Ibid.

12. Ibid.

13. Ibid.

14. G. S. Sparrow, *Lucid Dreaming: Dawning of the Clear Light* (Virginia Beach: A.R.E. Press 1976), 33.

15. Asklepios the Greek god of health was symbolized by the snake, and indeed, this creature was commonly associated with the god in cult and ritual. Whether or not Asklepios actually ever took the form of a snake (as did another light bearer), the two were strongly associated in ritual and myth.

16. P. Tholey, op. cit., 265.

17. P. Tholey, op. cit., 272.

18. H. Saint-Denys, op. cit.

19. Cf., S. Kaplan-Williams, *The Jungian Senoi Dreamwork Manual* (Berkeley: Journey Press, 1985).
    For more recommendations on various approaches and outcomes in lucid dream encounters with hostile dream figures, see P. Tholey, "A Model of Lucidity Training As a Means of Self-Healing and Psychological Growth," *Conscious Mind, Sleeping Brain*, eds. J. Gackenbach and S. LaBerge (New York: Plenum, 1988), 263–287.

6 Life as a Dream

1. I. Shah, *The Sufis* (London: Octagon Press, 1964), 141.

2. T. Tulku, *Openness Mind* (Berkeley, California: Dharma Press, 1978), 77.

3. Ibid., 90.

4. Ibid., 78.

5. Ibid., 86.

6. I. Shah, "Myself," *The Subtleties of the Inimitable Mulla Narsudin* (London: Octagon Press, 1983).

7. Ibid., 90.

8. S. LaBerge, *Lucid Dreaming* (Los Angeles: Jeremy P. Tarcher, Inc., 1985), 244–245.

9. I. Shah, *Seeker After Truth* (London: Octagon Press, 1982), 33.

10. S. LaBerge, "Lucid Dreaming: Directing the Action As It Happens," *Psychology Today* 15 (1981): 48–57.

11. W. James, *The Varieties of Religious Experience* (New York: Modern Library, 1929), 378–379.

12. R. de Becker, *The Understanding of Dreams* (London: Allen & Unwin, 1965), 406.

13. Ibid., 138.

14. Ibid.

15. A. R. Orage, *Psychological Exercises* (New York: Samuel Weiser, 1930), 92.

16. J. H. M. Whiteman, *The Mystical Life* (London: Faber & Faber, 1961), 57.

17. T. S. Eliot, 1940, "East Coker," *Four Quartets*.

18. I. Shah, *Thinkers of the East* (London: Octagon Press, 1971), 123.

About the Author

...

© ETHAN SPEELBERG

STEPHEN LABERGE, Ph.D., entered this world in 1947. As an Air Force brat, he saw much of the planet, and developed a keen interest in science as a means of understanding the cosmos. In 1967, he obtained his bachelor's degree in mathematics after two years at the University of Arizona, and began graduate studies in chemical physics at Stanford University. Following a hiatus spent in quest of the Holy Grail, he returned to Stanford and laid the groundwork for his pioneering breakthroughs in lucid-dreaming research, obtaining his Ph.D. in psychophysiology in 1980. Since then, he has been continuing work at Stanford studying lucid dreaming and psychophysiological correlates of states of consciousness. In 1988, acting on his conviction that lucid dreaming offers many benefits to humanity, Dr. LaBerge founded the Lucidity Institute, the mission of which is to advance research on the nature and potentials of consciousness and to apply the results of this research to the enhancement of human health and well-being. Email: st@lucidity.com

SOUNDS TRUE was founded in 1985, with a clear vision: to disseminate spiritual wisdom. Located in Boulder, Colorado, Sounds True publishes teaching programs that are designed to educate, uplift, and inspire. We work with many of the leading spiritual teachers, thinkers, healers, and visionary artists of our time.

To see our full catalog of tools and teachings for personal and spiritual transformation, please visit SoundsTrue.com.